Figure It Out!
WORKBOOK

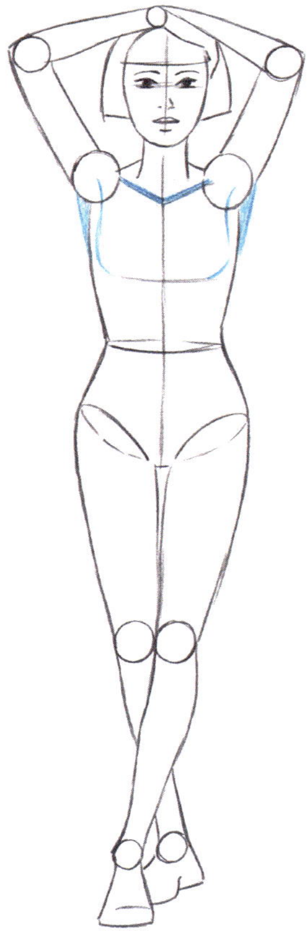

Get Creative 6

DRAWING WITH Christopher Hart

An imprint of
Mixed Media Resources
104 West 27th Street
New York, NY 10001

Editorial Director
JOAN KRELLENSTEIN

Editor
LAURA COOKE

Art Director
IRENE LEDWITH

Assistant Editor
JACOB SEIFERT

Layout
JENNIFER MARKSON

Production
J. ARTHUR MEDIA

Vice President
TRISHA MALCOLM

Publisher
CAROLINE KILMER

Production Manager
DAVID JOINNIDES

President
ART JOINNIDES

Chairman
JAY STEIN

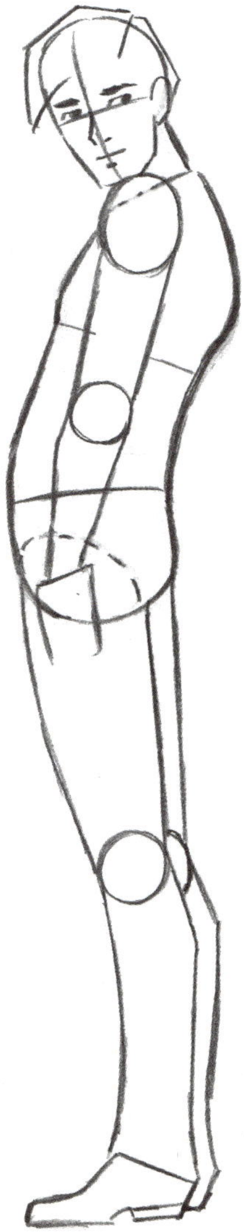

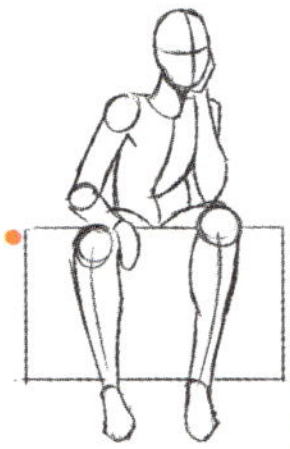

Library of Congress Cataloging-in-Publication data
Hart, Christopher, 1957-author.
The figure it out workbook : a step-by-step guide to figure drawing / by Christopher Hart. — First edition. | New York : Drawing with Christopher Hart, 2018.
ISBN 9781640210110 (pbk.)
LCSH: Figure drawing--Technique. | Human figure in art.
LCC NC765 .H195 2018 | DDC 743.4--dc23
2017027363

Manufactured in China

1 3 5 7 9 10 8 6 4 2

First Edition

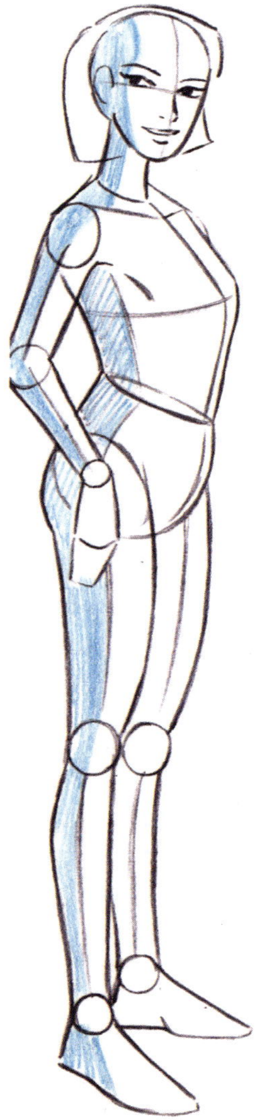

Figure It Out! WORKBOOK

INTRODUCTION

The ability to draw the head and figure is an essential skill for artists of all levels, especially beginners. This workbook gives emerging artists the practical tips and techniques needed to make figure drawing fun and satisfying. The concepts are easy to grasp, and the instructions are clear. Each step-by-step lesson builds on the previous one so that you gain momentum as you progress through the workbook. All the fundamentals of figure drawing are provided, including the correct proportions of the head and body along with how to draw the features of the face, the figure at various angles, the basic contours of the body, natural poses, hands, and more. With this workbook, you will get up to speed quickly, so you can begin to draw the human figure with confidence.

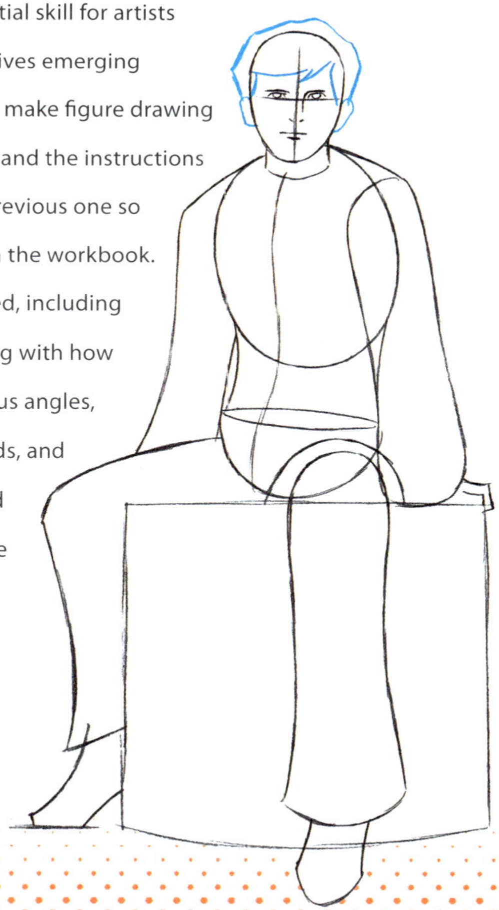

DRAWING THE HEAD

BE AN EGGHEAD: THE BASIC HEAD SHAPE

In order to place the features correctly and end up with a realistic-looking head, we need to start with a good shape. And it has to be one that can be easily reproduced at many angles. A circle is just too cartoony for a realistic drawing of the head, but an egg shape is very close. We'll need to make some minor modifications to this basic shape, but it works as a starting point.

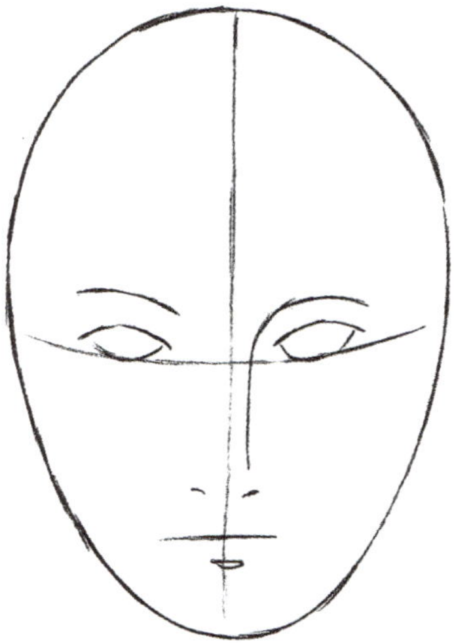

Front View

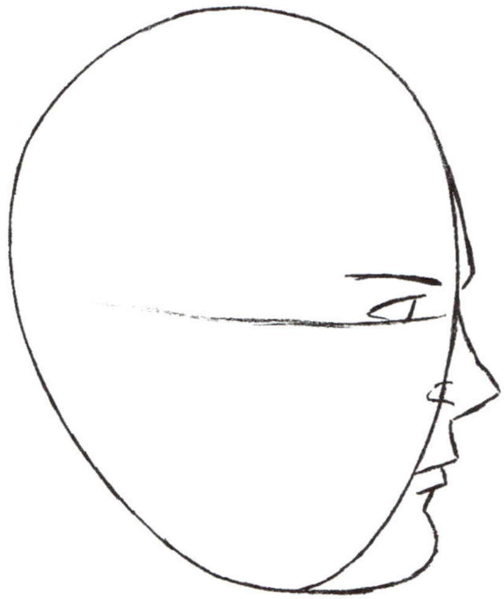

Profile

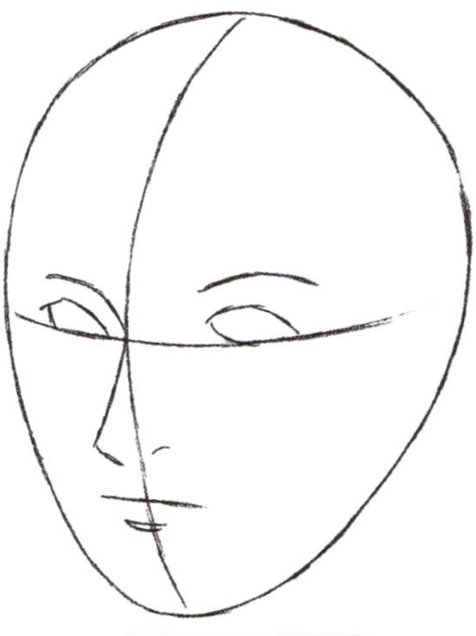

¾ View (left)

Notice how the egg shape tilts slightly to the left in ¾ view.

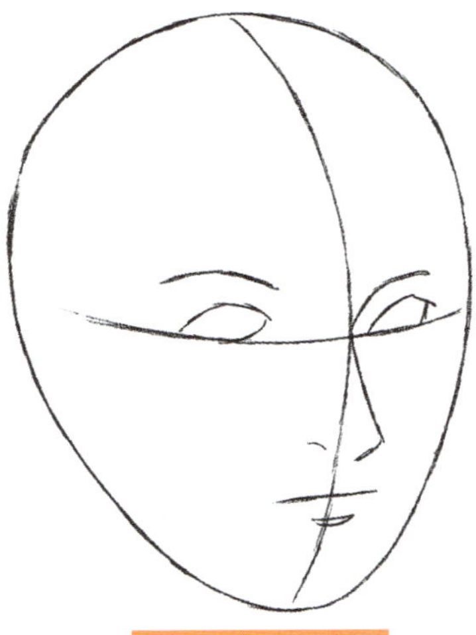

¾ View (right)

Notice how the egg shape tilts slightly to the right in ¾ view.

YOU TRY IT!

Practice drawing the basic oval head shape, with rough features, from all directions in the space below. Keep it simple.

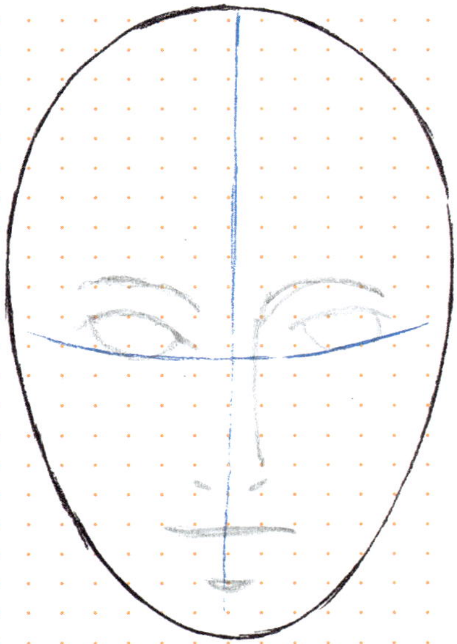

Front View

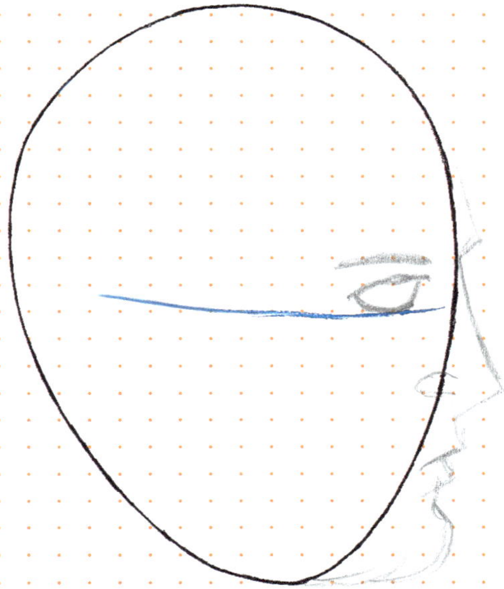

Profile

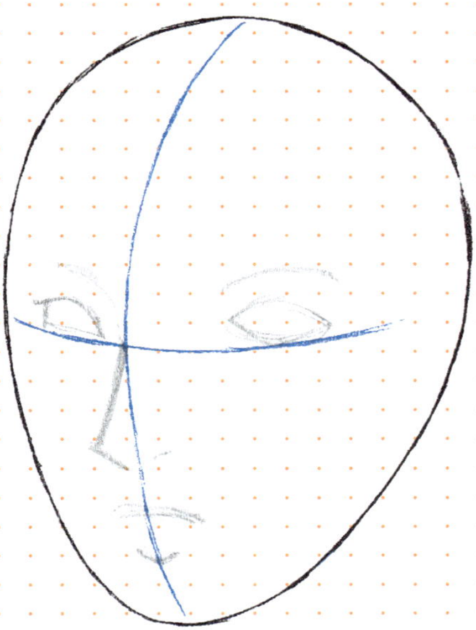

¾ View (left)

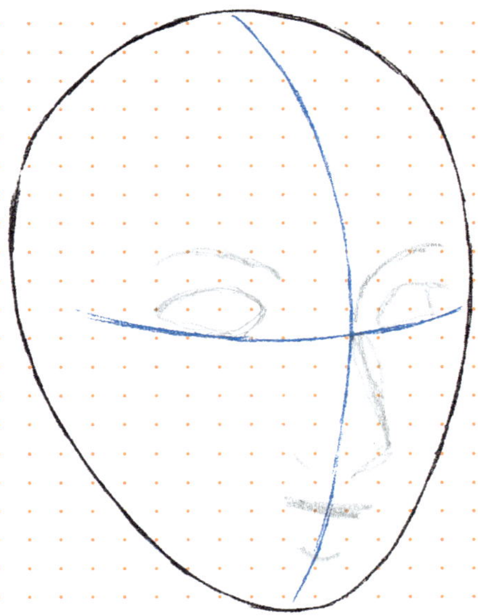

¾ View (right)

SCULPT THE HEAD

Now that we have the basic outline of the head, we need to sculpt it to make it more closely resemble an actual head. Happily, all that's required are a few minor adjustments.

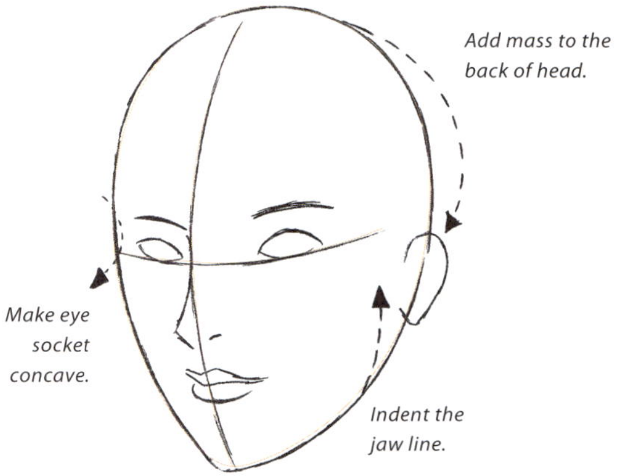

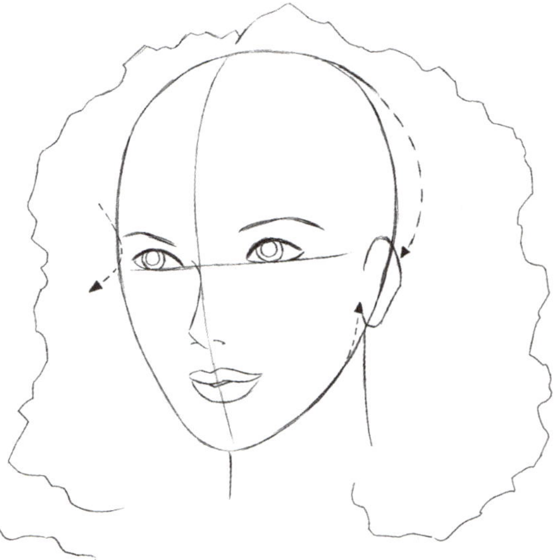

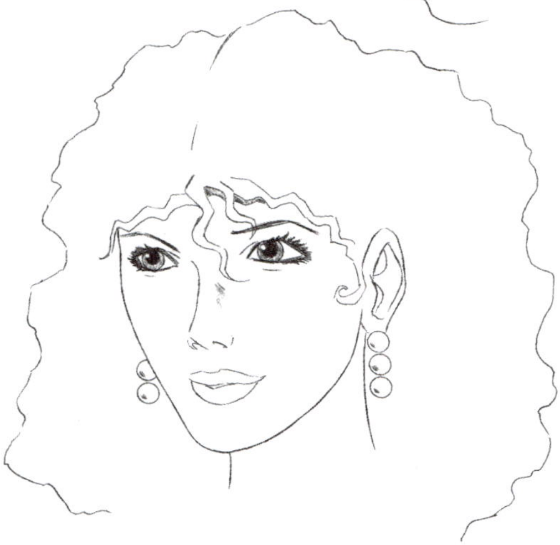

Head Shape: Male vs. Female

Here's a hint that will help make your characters look more feminine or more masculine. When the male head is posed in a ¾ view, there are "bumps" on the far side of the face—the cheekbone, the cheek muscle, and the chin. You can eliminate the cheek muscle in females for a sleeker, more feminine appearance.

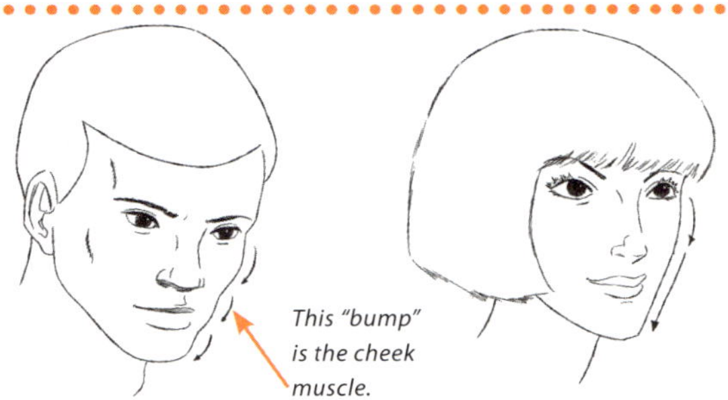

YOU TRY IT!

Practice "sculpting" the basic egghead shape in the space below by making small adjustments to the outline.

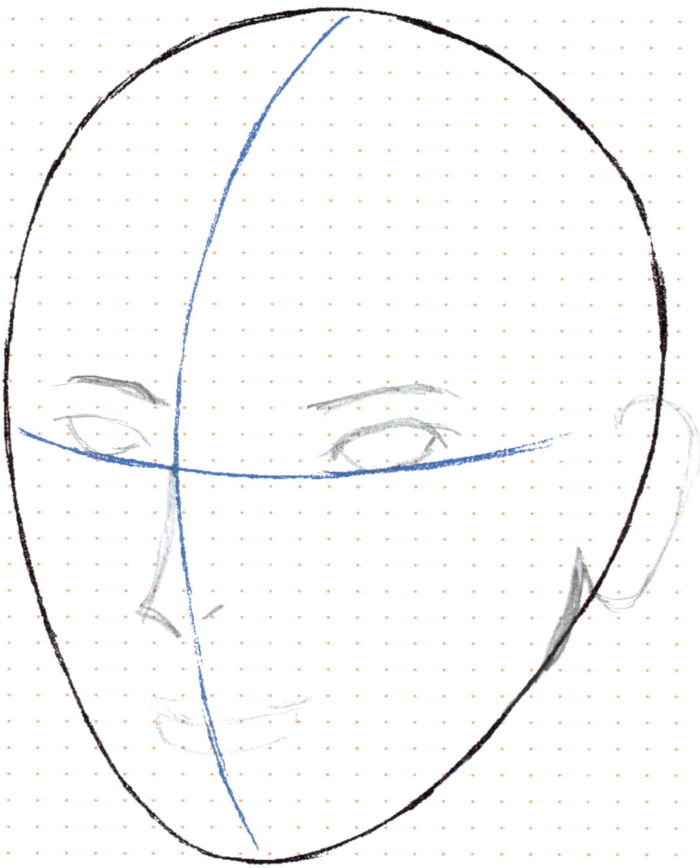

THE EYES

The eyes are arguably the most important features of the face when drawing the head, because they appear close to the middle of the head and because they're so expressive. Vary the tone (darkness) of the pupil, iris, eyebrow, and eyelids to bring the eyes forward. The lines of the eyelids are usually drawn darker than the other lines of the face.

COMMON EYE SHAPES

There are as many types of eyes as there are people who have eyes. However, for drawing purposes, there are three basic shapes for men and three common types for women.

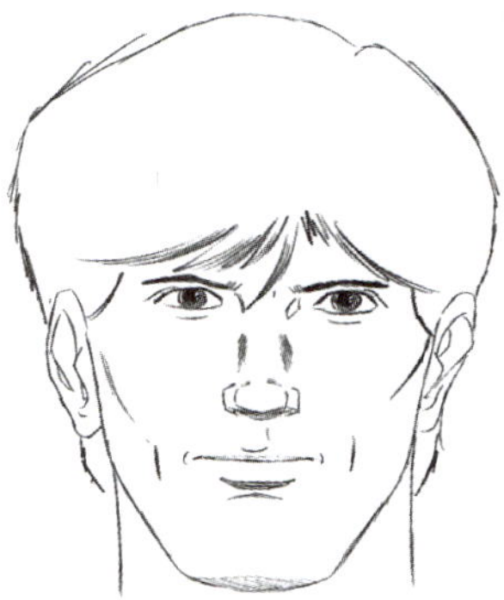

Male Eyes

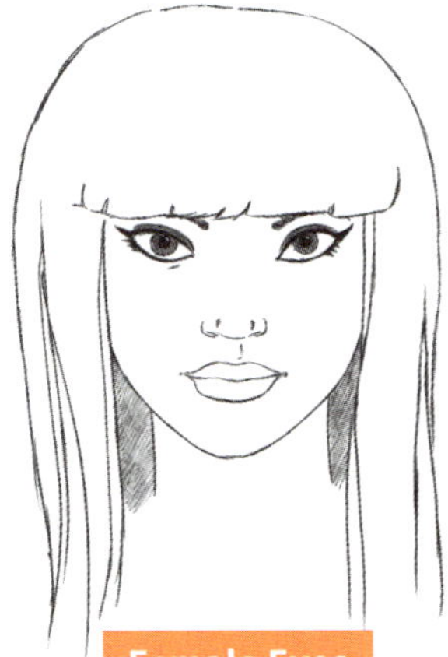

Female Eyes

You can't go wrong with ***almond-shaped*** *eyes. They're expressive and look correct on most facial types.*

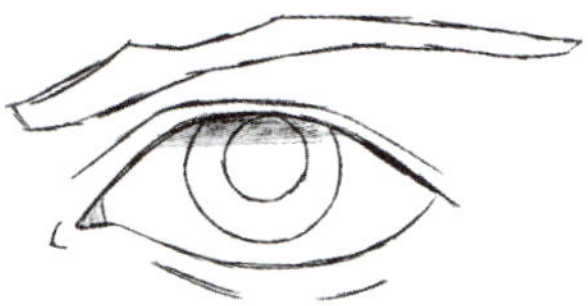

The ***almond-shaped eye*** *has a subtle curve to the top eyelid that is emphasized by the sweep of the eyelashes.*

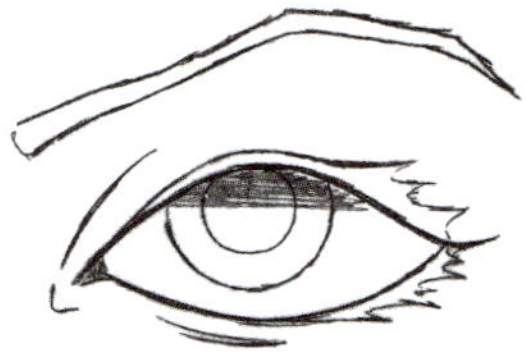

Rectangular eyes *are masculine and work well on square-jawed guys.*

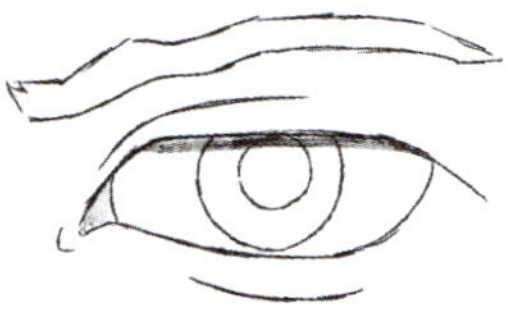

The ***slender eye*** *hides more of the pupil underneath the top eyelid for a sexy look.*

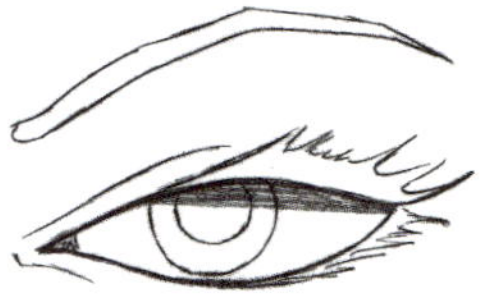

Droopy eyes *are common on middle-aged men.*

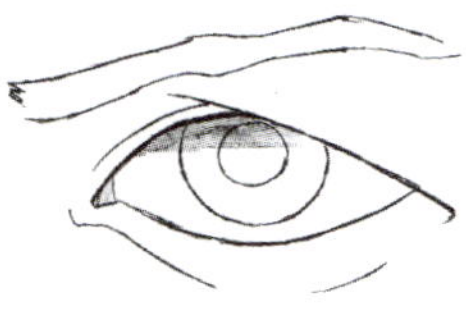

Round eyes *are a cute, pert look. Feather the eyelashes around the eye.*

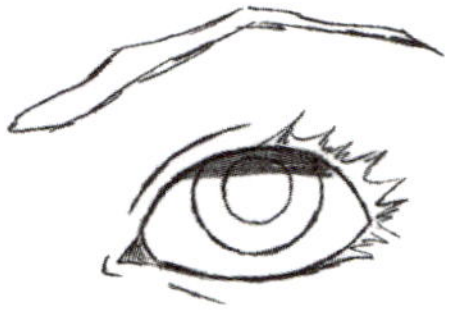

YOU TRY IT!

Practice drawing male and female eye shapes in the space below.

THE NOSE AND MOUTH

I like to think of the nose and mouth as a unit because the nose anchors the mouth in place. Match up the bottom of the nose with the "cupid's bow" of the lips (the depression in the middle of the upper lip) to get the alignment right. Here are a few practice examples of noses and lips at various angles.

MEN

When drawing men, you can usually add more detail to the nose than when drawing women.

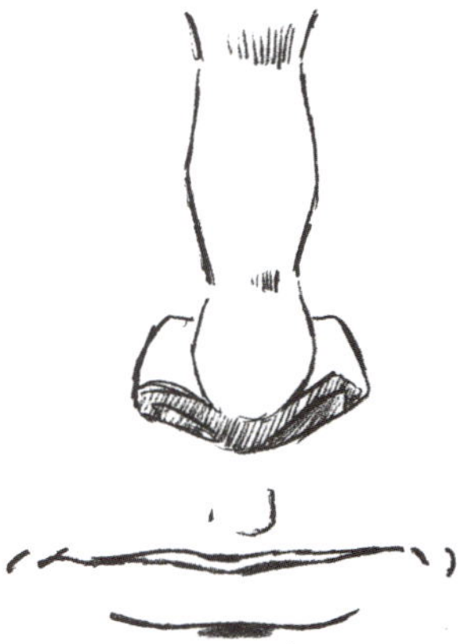

Front View

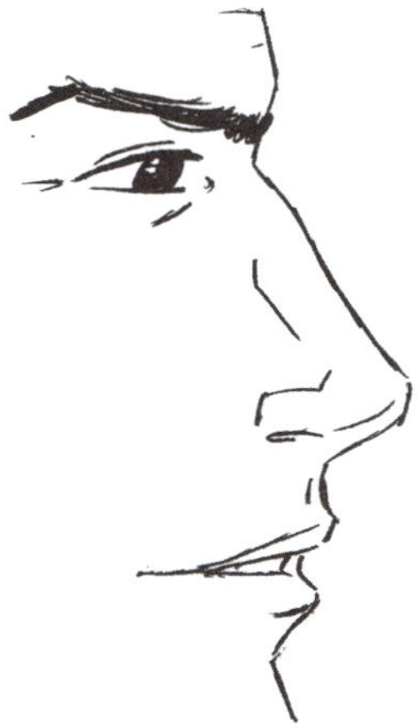

Profile

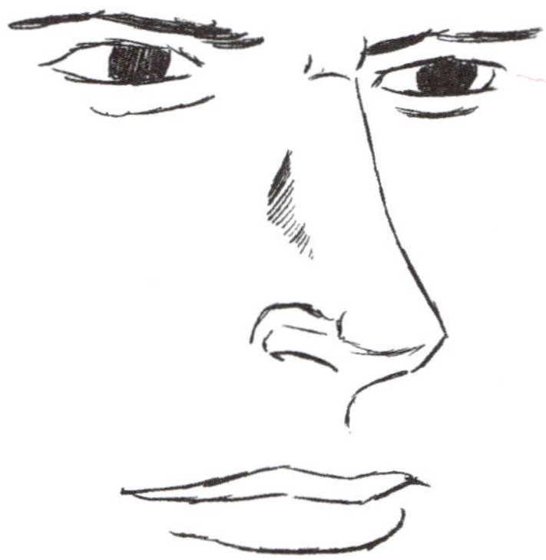

¾ Right View

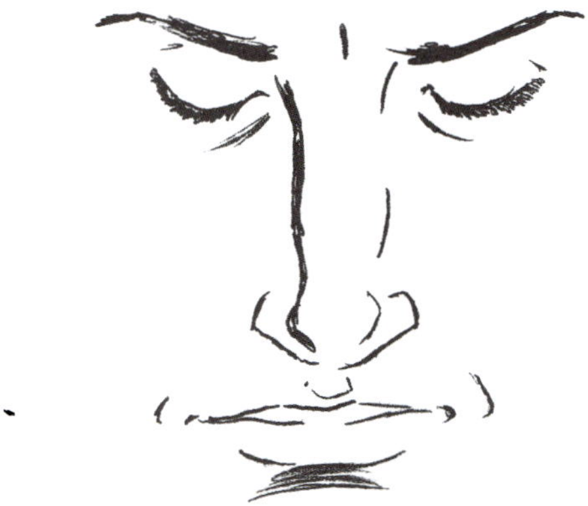

Down Angle

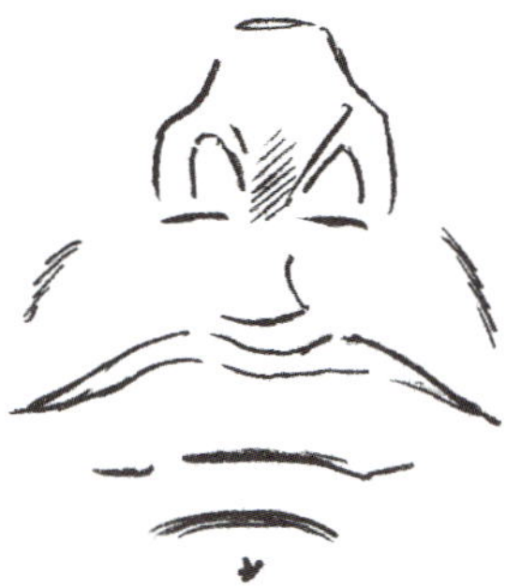

Up Angle

YOU TRY IT!

Practice drawing male noses from several directions in the space below.

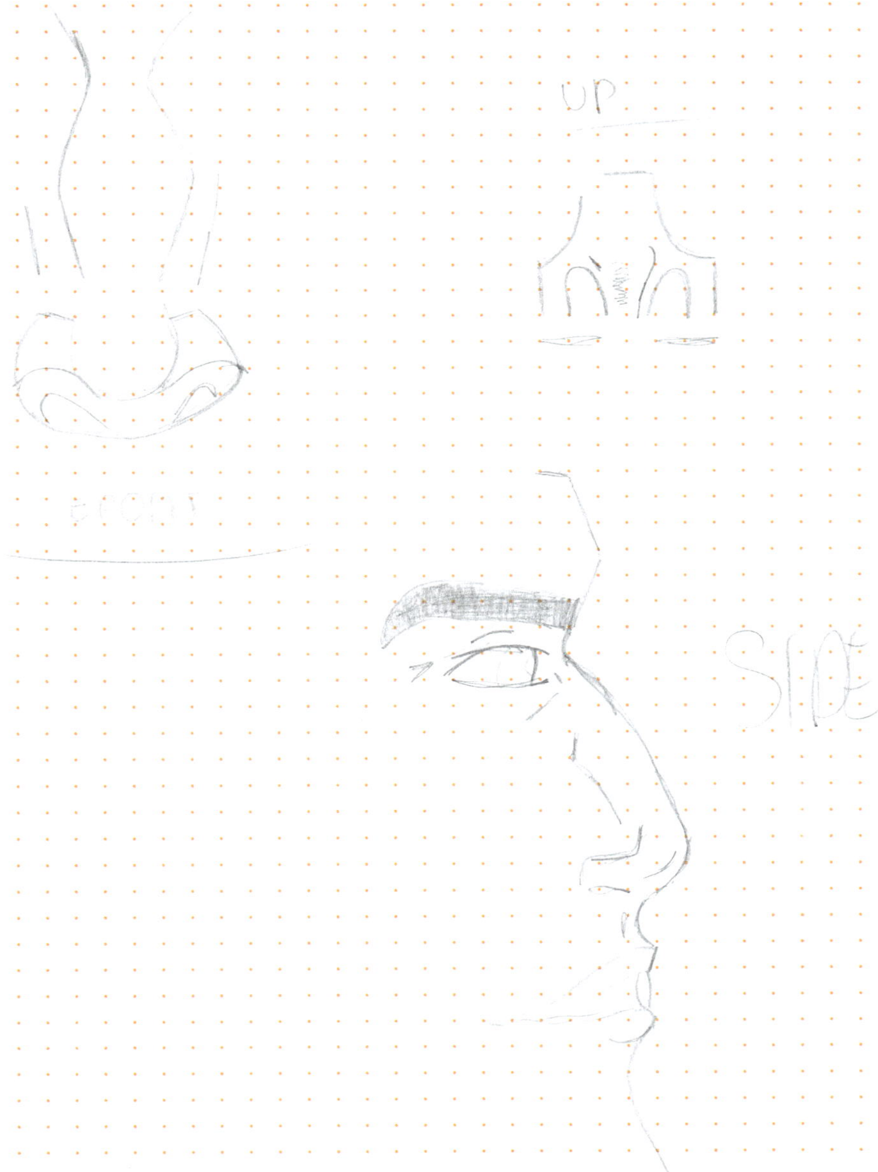

WOMEN

The idealized female nose is actually quite easy to draw, because you leave out most of the lines! The more detailed the nose, the less feminine it looks. So use fewer lines and let the viewer's eye connect the missing ones to flesh out the image. Try to use softer, sweeping curves, without hard angles. And keep the tip of the nose small.

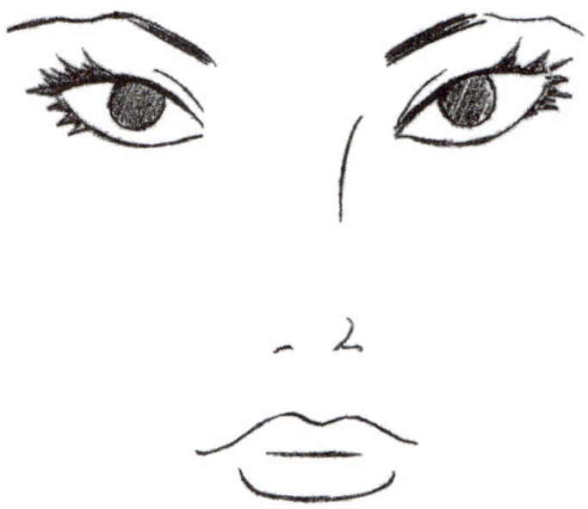

Front View

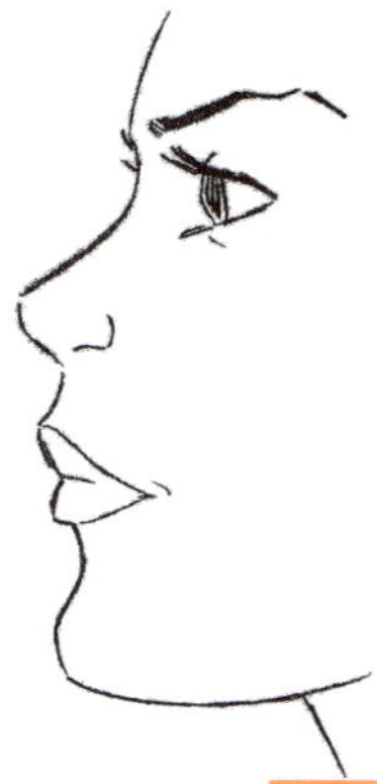

Profile

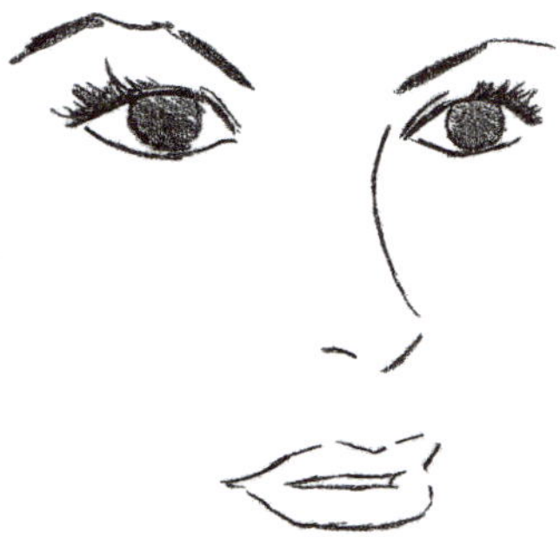

¾ Right View

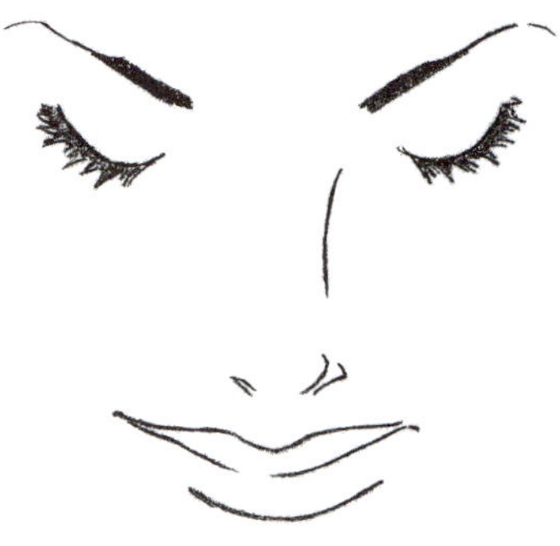

Down Angle

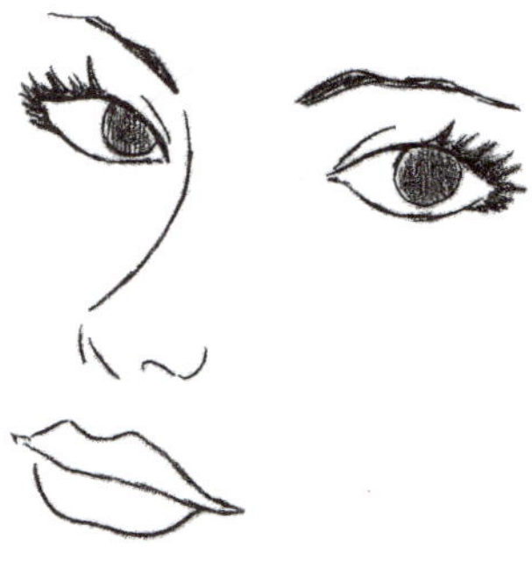

¾ Left View, Up

YOU TRY IT!

Practice drawing female noses from several directions in the space below.

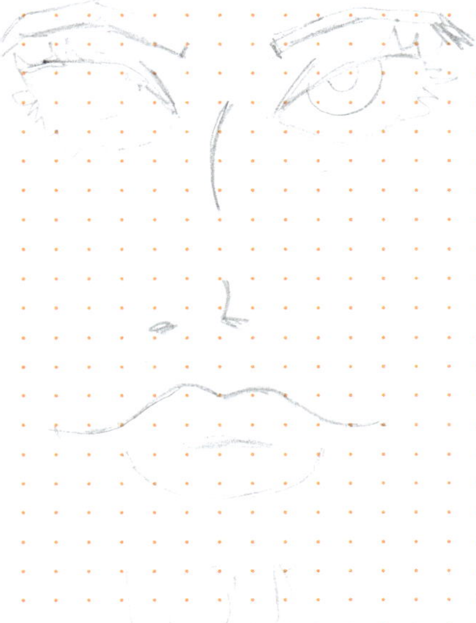

THE EARS

Ears are basically unisex. Male and female ears are interchangeable in shape, although female ears are usually smaller. And a woman's ears are often hidden by her hair, making them even easier to draw!

FRONT VIEW

The ears don't stick straight out to the sides, flapping like a cartoon. Nor are they pasted to the sides of the head. They're somewhere in between.

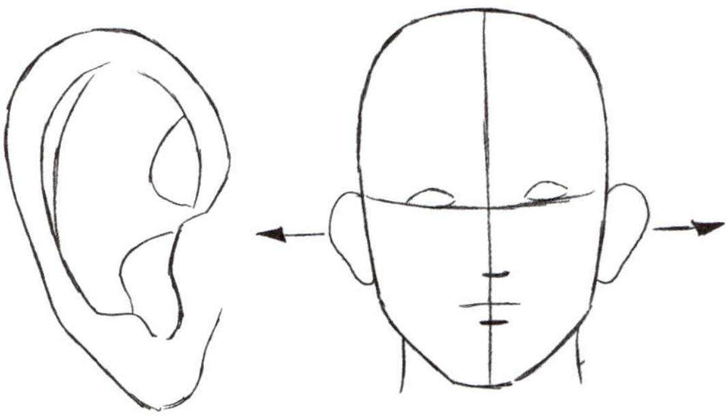

Wrong!

Ears stick straight out, making the character look goofy.

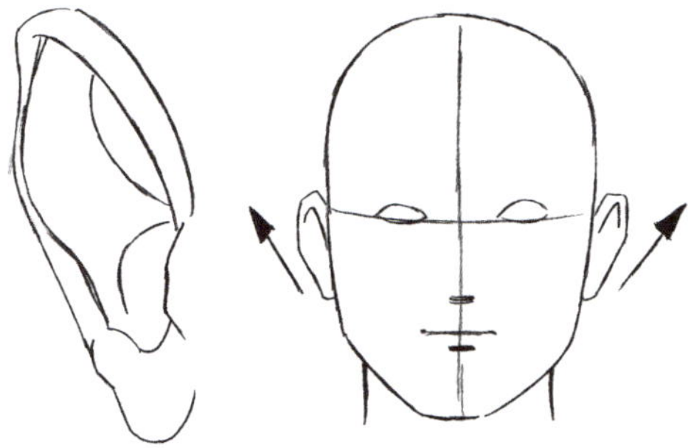

Right!

Ears angled back and away from the head

REAR VIEW

There are two ways to draw the ears when viewing a person from behind.

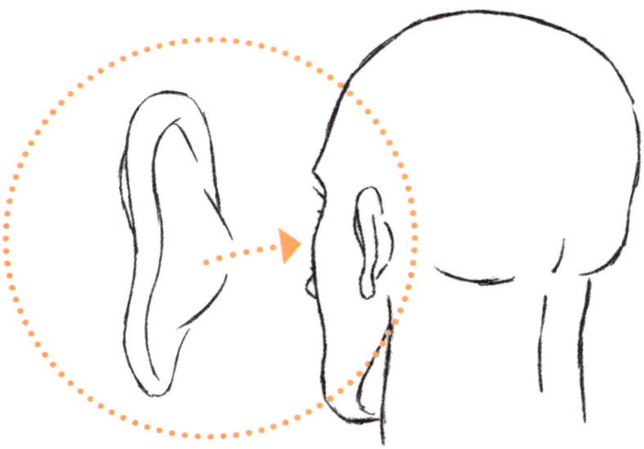

Method 1

In this view, we see very little of the face, and therefore, we see more of the "cup" of the ear.

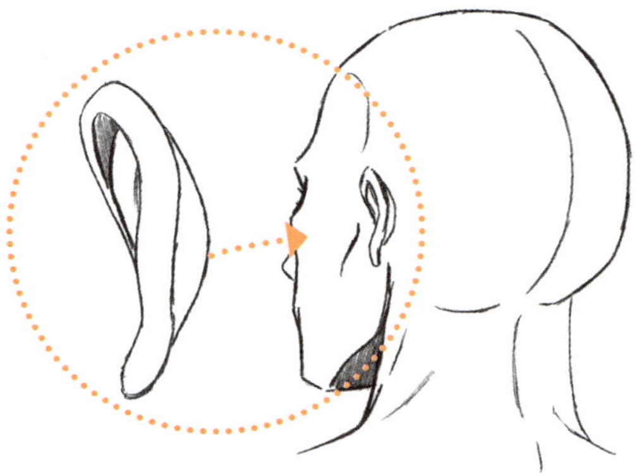

Method 2

Here we see a little more of the face. Therefore, we see a bit of the interior of the ear as it winds around and loops back into itself.

YOU TRY IT!

Practice drawing ears from the front and rear views in the space.

JAW SHAPES

The jaw is basically a U shape that cups the bottom of the head. You adjust the shape of the jaw to enhance the character type. For example, you can convey the look of an athletic guy with a square jaw, whereas a meek character may look more convincing with a subtler jaw shape.

SQUARE

The angles of the chin occur low on the face.

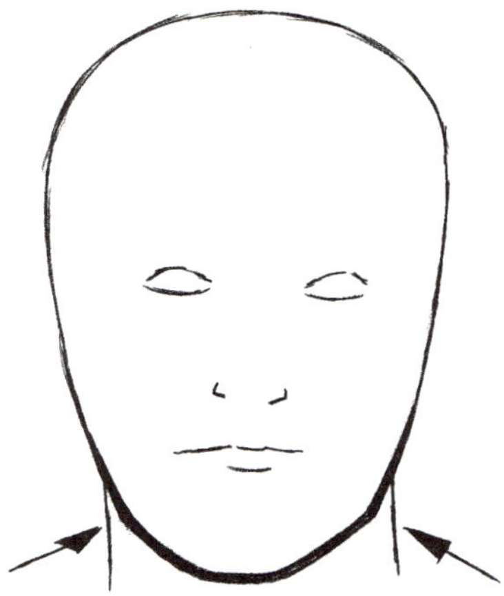

SCULPTED

This is a sleeker look, with sharp angles carved out of the head.

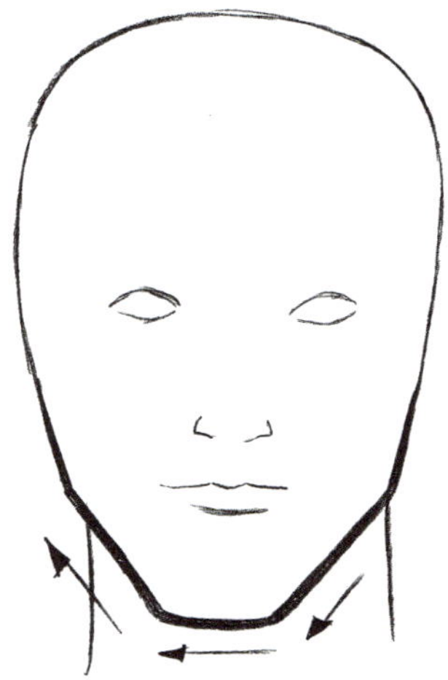

ROUND

This is a pleasing look, without any angular break. Softer lines create this jaw in the shape of a giant U.

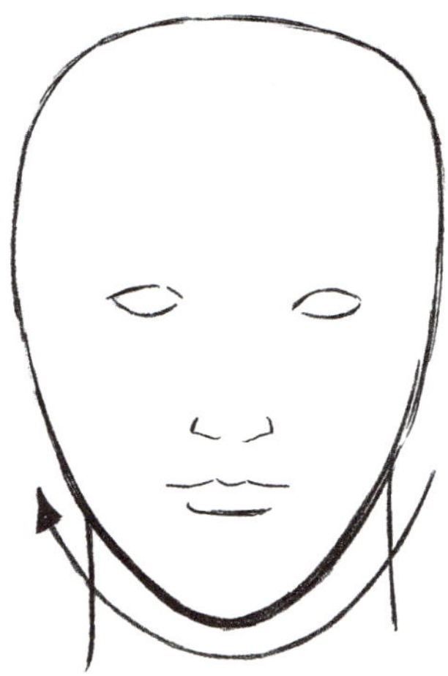

YOU TRY IT!

Practice drawing jaw shapes on the face below. In the final image, practice drawing all features.

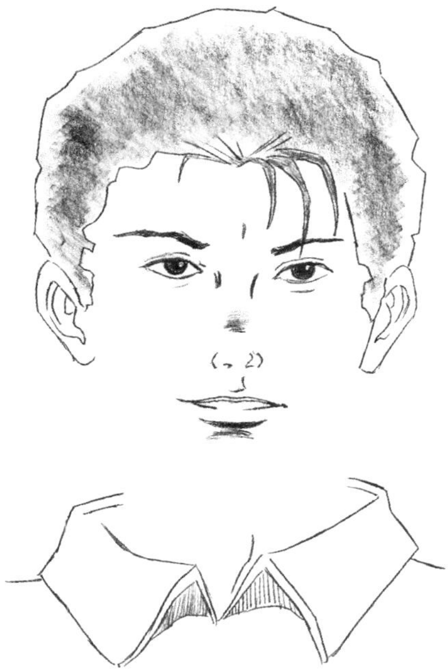

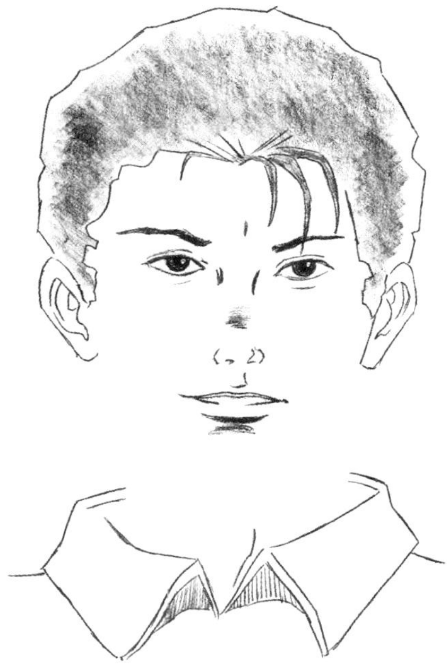

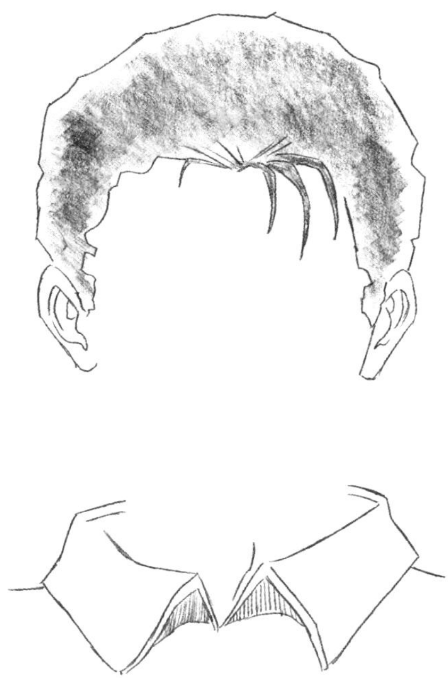

THE CHIN (IT'S A MUSCLE!)

The chin is actually a muscle. It can move up and down depending on the person's expression. Visualize the chin as a ball that has been cut in half and pasted on the face. That will make it easier to turn the head at various angles and maintain the semi-spherical chin shape. A woman's chin is not nearly as pronounced as a man's.

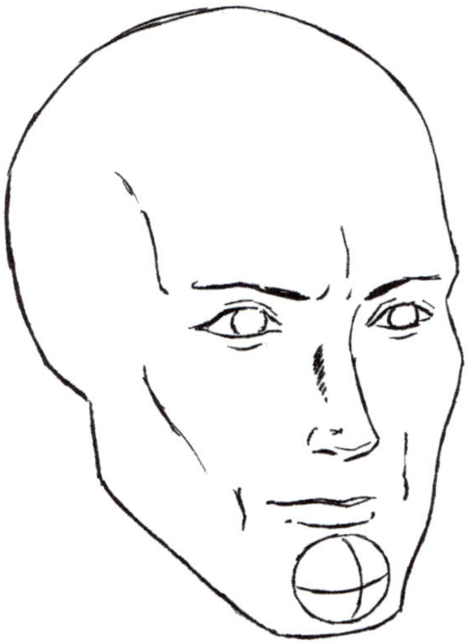

¾ View

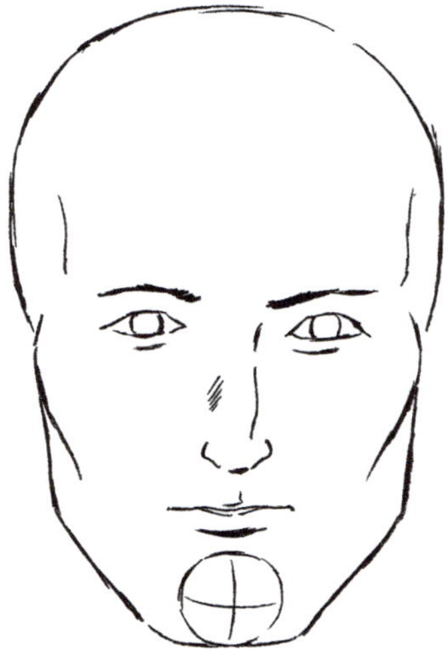

Front View

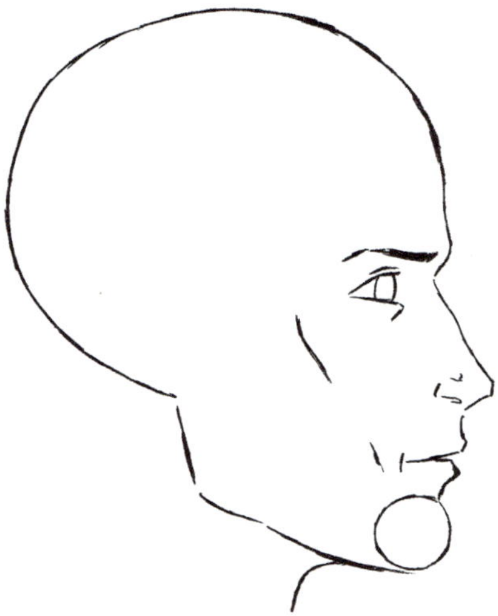

Profile

YOU TRY IT!

Practice drawing the chin muscle from different views on the basic face shapes in the space below. After you've correctly drawn the chin, try to fill out the rest of the face.

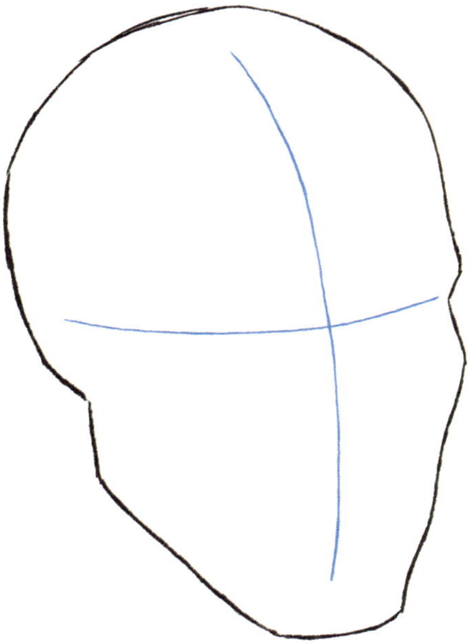

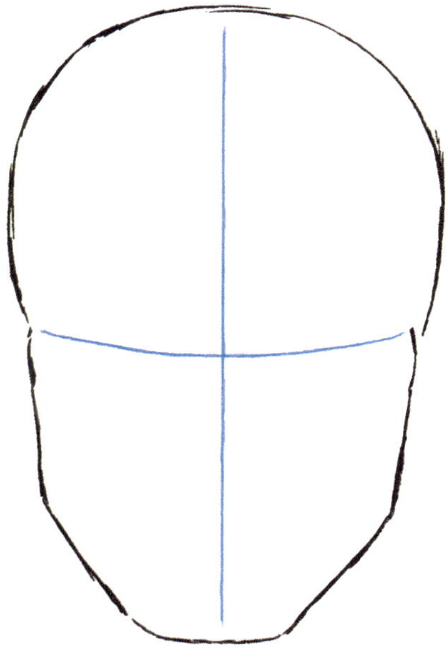

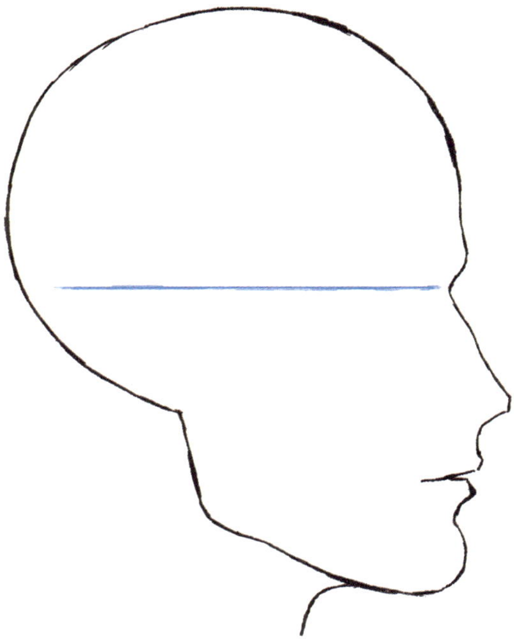

THE HEAD AND NECK AS A UNIT

The head and neck work as one unit; the position of one will always affect the other. When the head tilts, twists, or turns, it puts stress on the neck. We can show this in a variety of ways.

HEAD TILT—SIDE TO SIDE

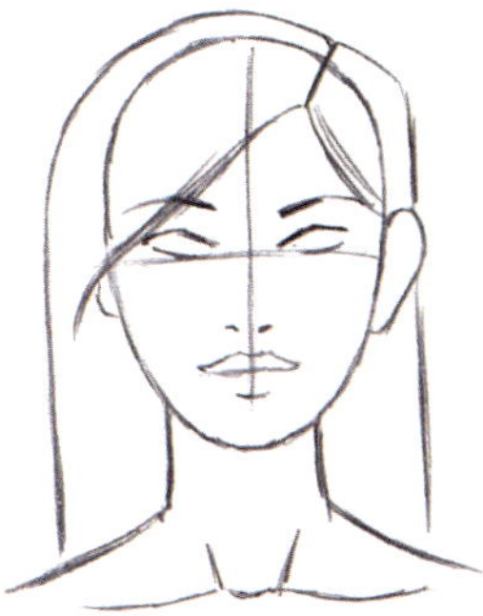

Neutral

Symmetrical

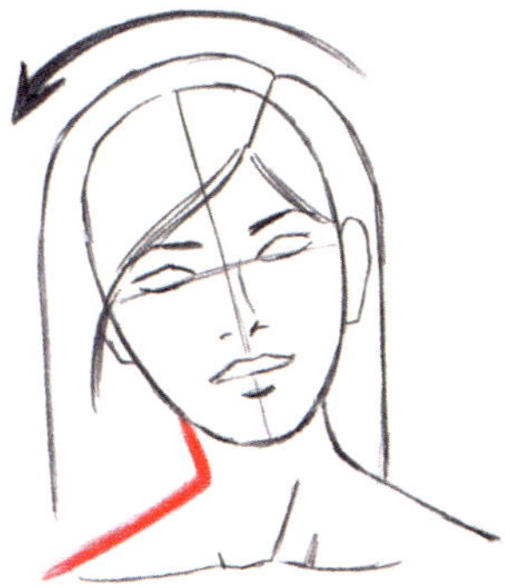

Tilts Left

When the head tilts left, the neck crimps on the left side.

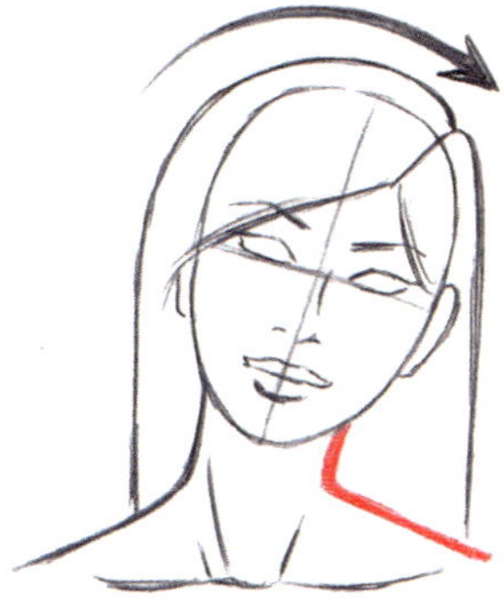

Tilts Right

When the head tilts right, the neck crimps on the right side.

HEAD TILT—FORWARD AND BACKWARD

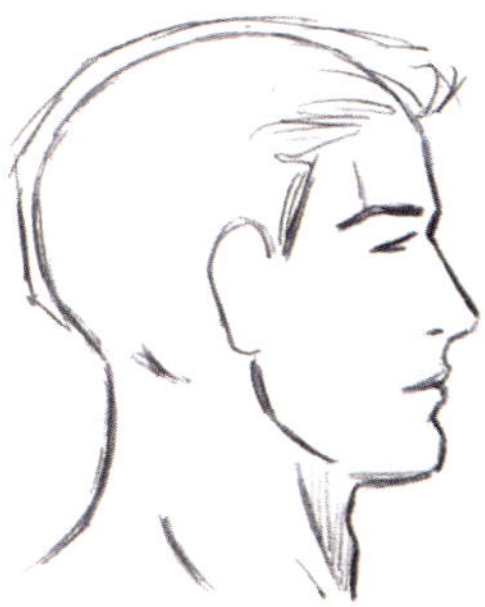

Neutral

Symmetrical

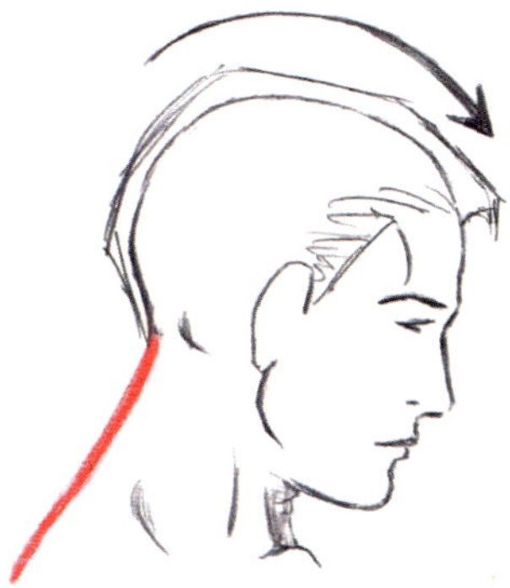

Tilts Forward

When the head tilts forward, the back of the neck and the upper back blend to create a single line, which gives the appearance of length.

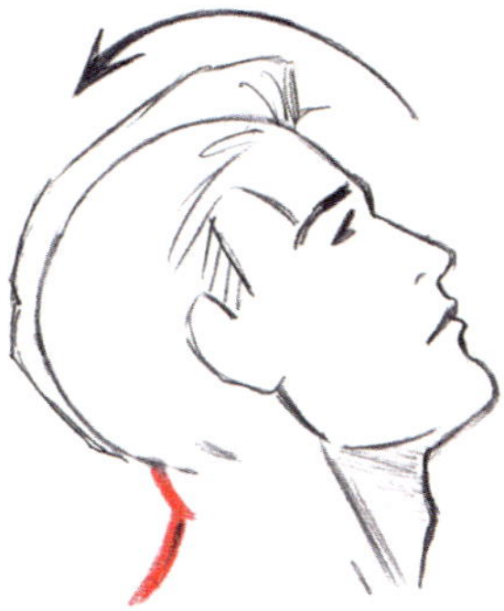

Tilts Back

When the head tilts back, the back of the neck crimps, which gives the appearance of a shorter line.

YOU TRY IT!

Practice drawing different tilts of the neck in relation to the head in the space below.

CHECK YOUR PROPORTIONS

You know how you sometimes work hard to get a drawing just right, then you look over the final product only to realize that—yikes!—your proportions are out of whack? Kiss those dark days goodbye. You'll now be able to check your proportions at the initial sketch phase to make sure they're right. There are certain guidelines for idealized proportions that, when followed, produce a convincing drawing.* I call them "guidelines" rather than "rules" because everything can be reinterpreted according to your personal taste.

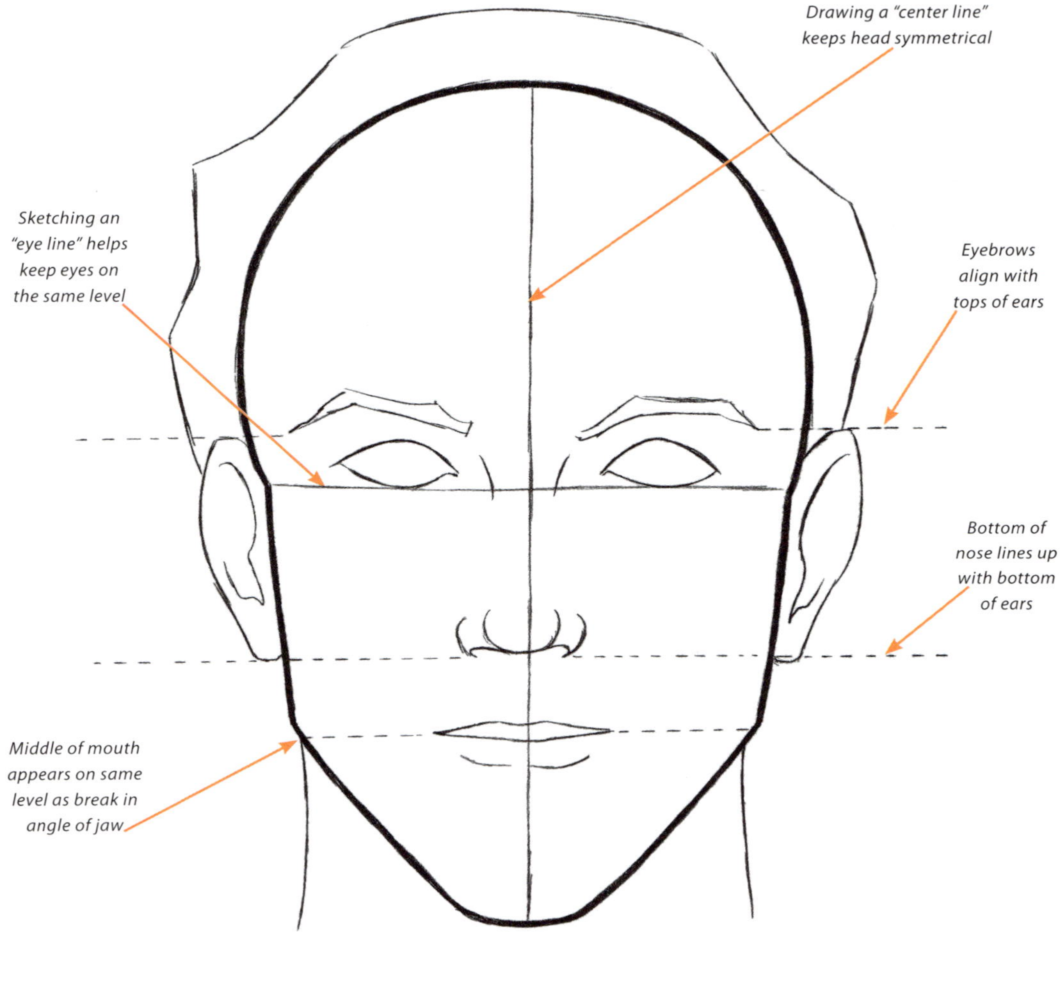

*See my book, *Figure It Out: Human Proportions*, for more in-depth information on drawing features proportionally.

YOU TRY IT!

Use the blank face outline below to draw guidelines and features that are in proper proportion to one another.

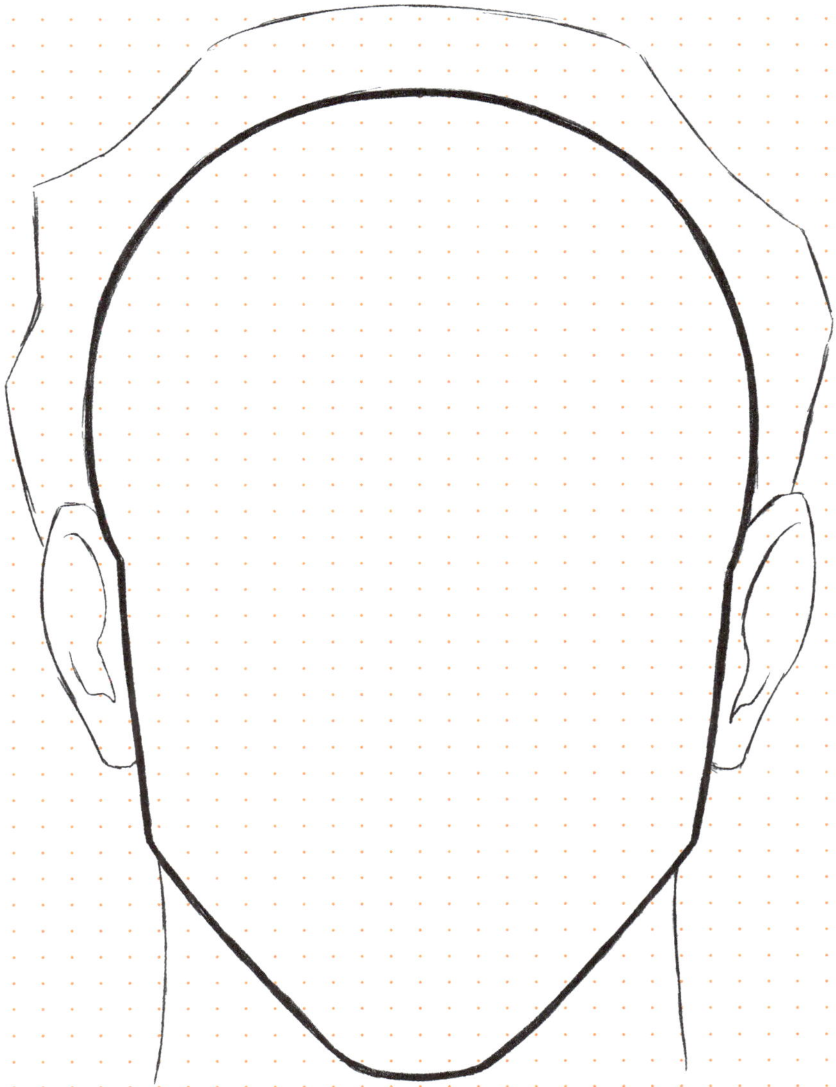

EXPRESSIONS

Now we're going to go back to the basic egg shape we began with and twist and tug its simple features in a few different directions. This will result in a series of classic expressions and attitudes that will be useful as we begin to draw more detailed faces.

Pleased

Corners of mouth turn up, pupils get bigger, and eyebrows arch.

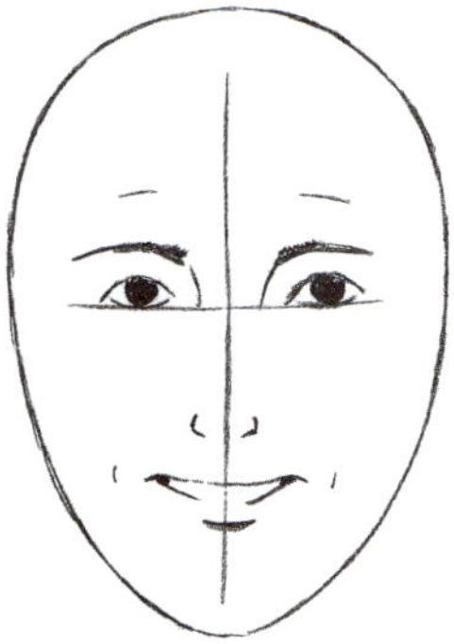

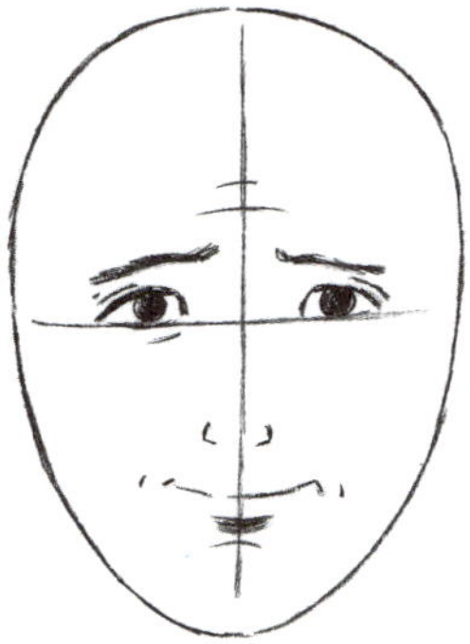

Sympathetic

Upturned eyebrows and a small smile

Scared

Eyes show lots of "white" and mouth compresses

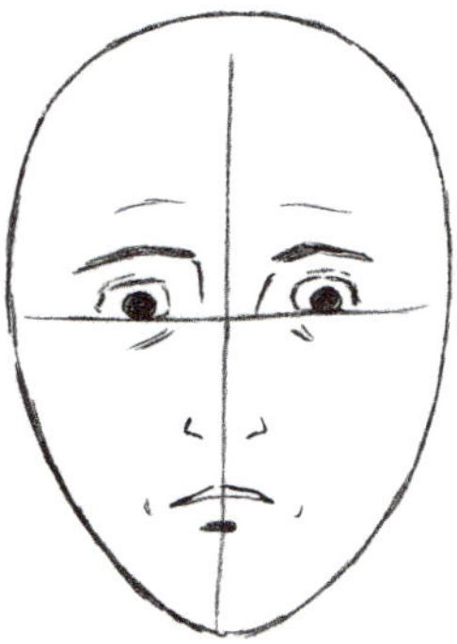

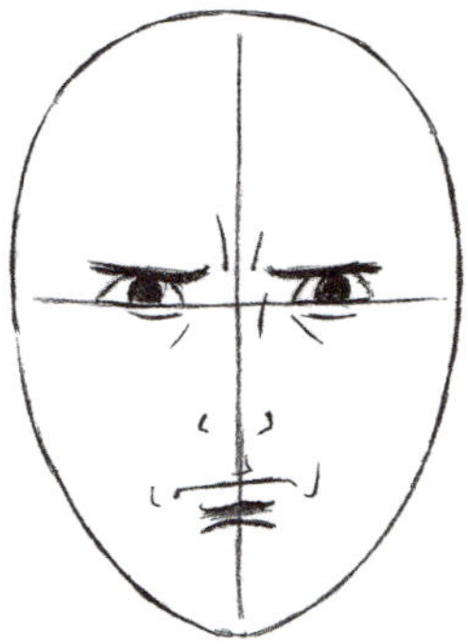

Angry

Eyebrows crush down on eyes, and lips press together in a hard line

Joyful

Squinty eyes and a broad smile

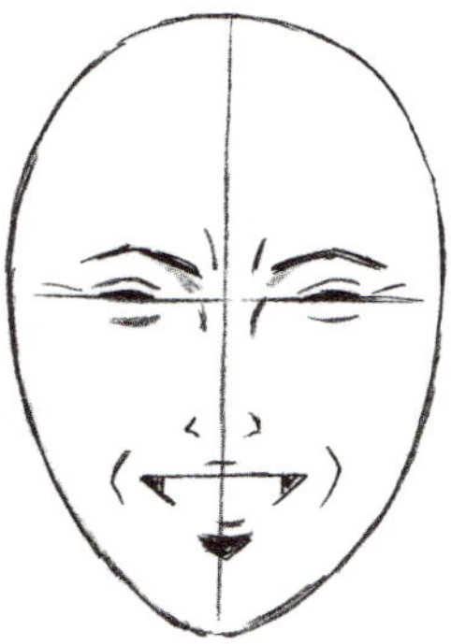

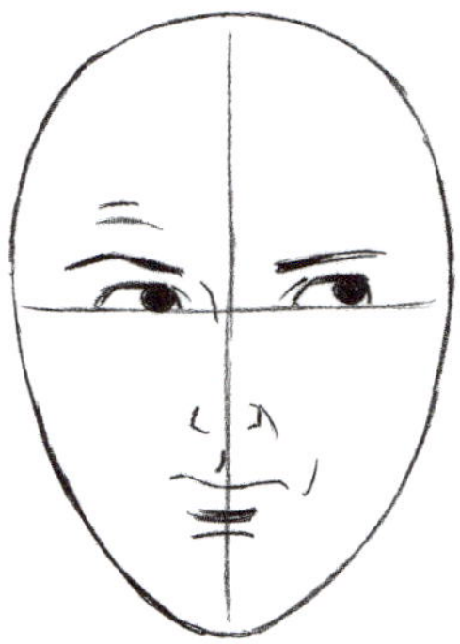

Skeptical

Sideways glance with pursed lips and one high arching eyebrow

YOU TRY IT!

Practice drawing the basic expressions above on the blank face shapes below. First, sketch the guidelines.

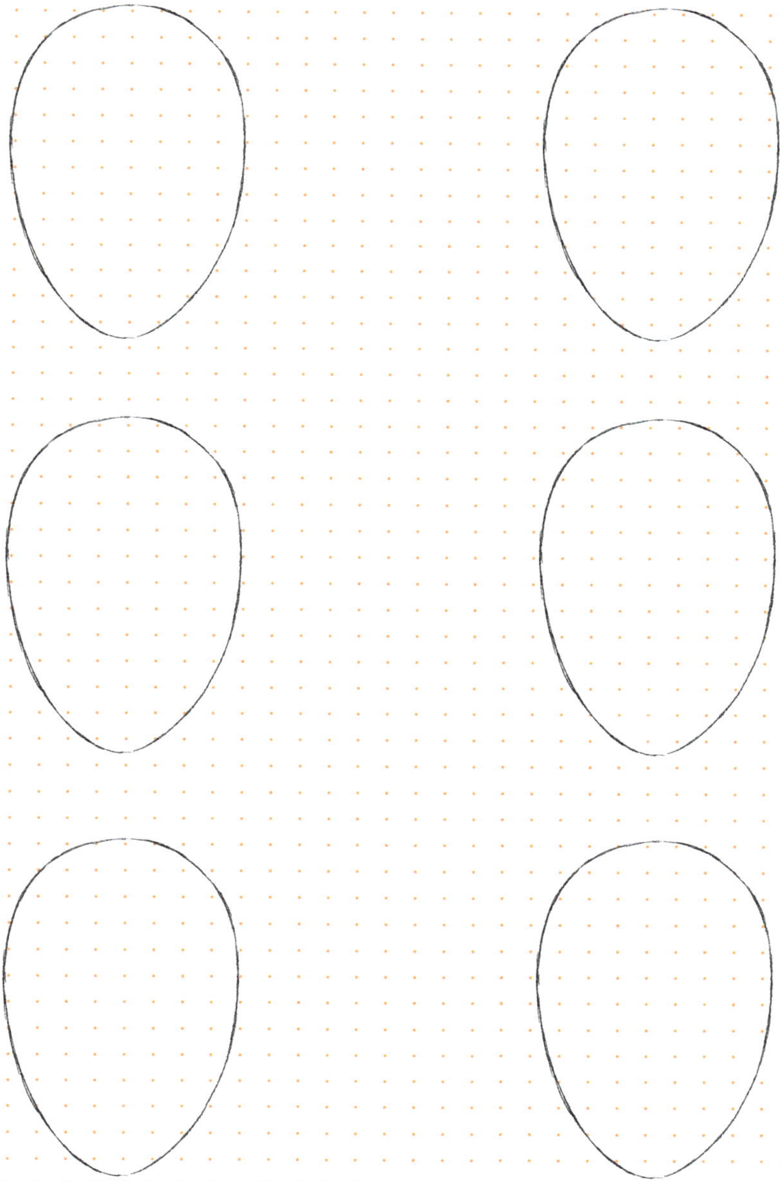

Blank pages for freehand sketching

STEP-BY-STEP HEADS

FRONT VIEW—MALE FACE

Now that we've covered the basics, we'll put it all together by drawing a variety of heads from start to finish. Don't feel that your drawings have to look just like mine. It's the general proportions and principles that should guide you.

In the front view, everything is symmetrical and open to view. Therefore, it's important to take a step back at the sketch phase to make sure all of the features are in balance and correctly aligned. This smiling young man has a wide face, but a narrow chin. Note how the symmetry of the face is held in place by the use of sketch guidelines.

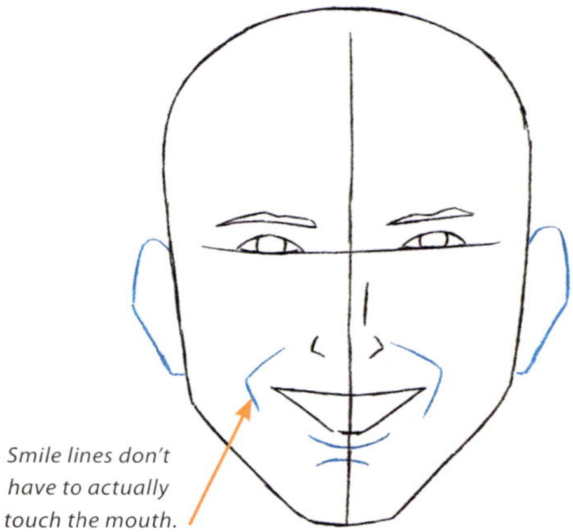

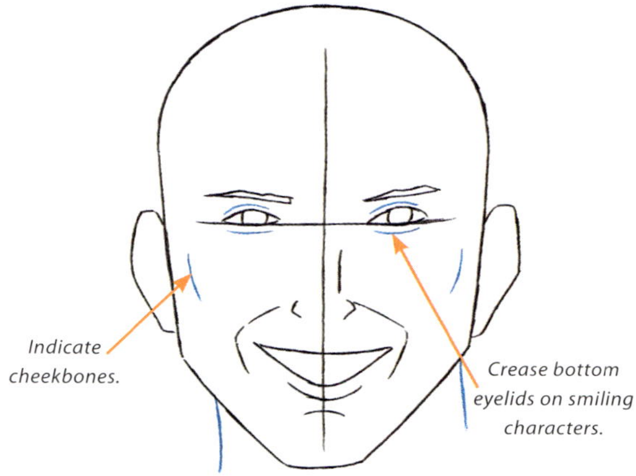

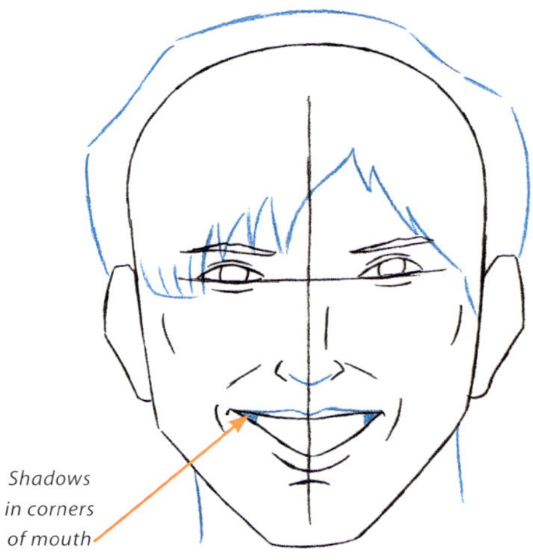

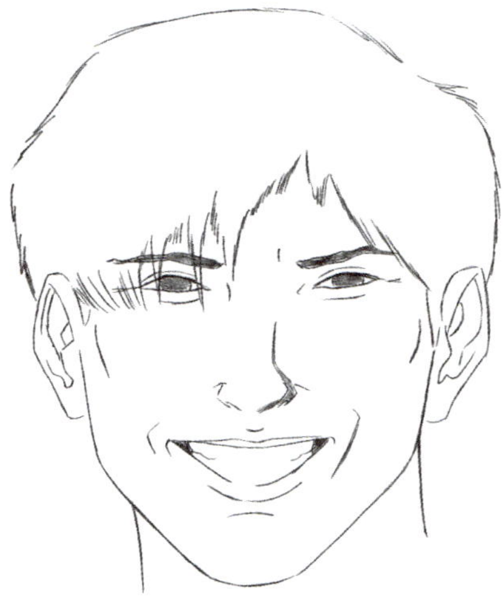

Did you know that the pupils actually expand when a person is happy?

YOU TRY IT!

Use the basic head shape below as a guide to practice drawing the face with a detailed expression.

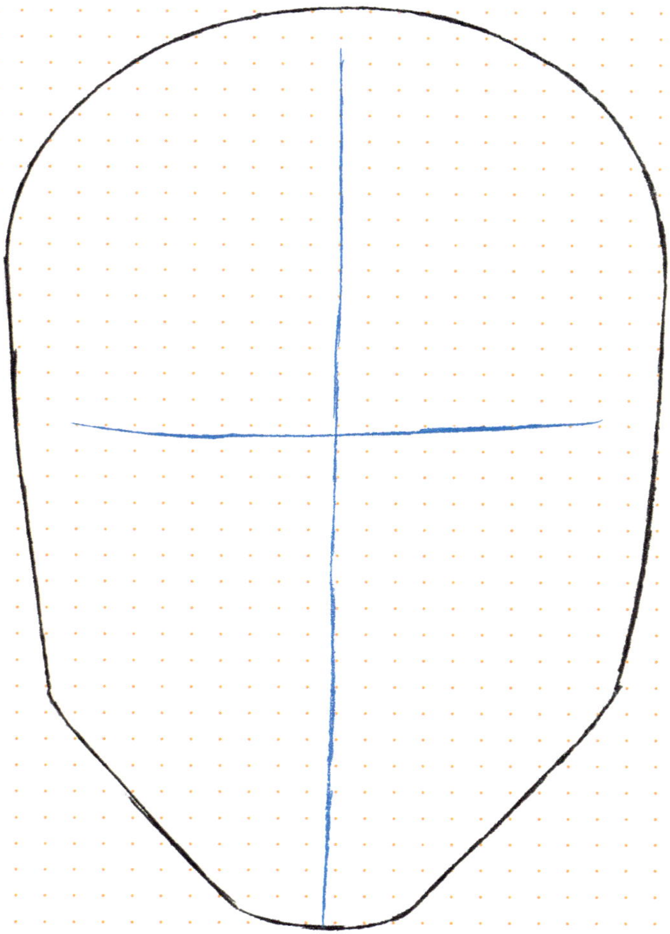

Hint

When a person smiles, the bottom eyelids crease and push up on the eyes, making them narrower.

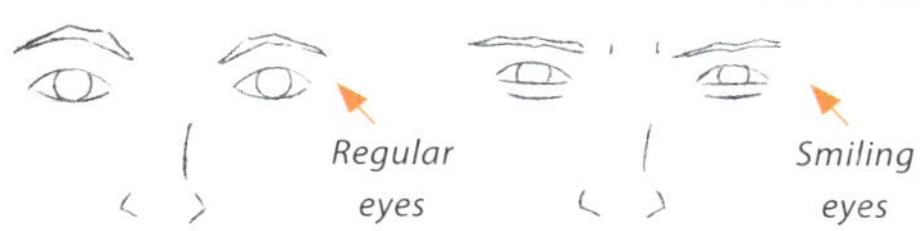

FRONT VIEW—FEMALE FACE

For the female face, focus on the symmetry of her features. Make sure the eyes and eyebrows line up evenly. And be sure the lips align with the middle of the nose and that the ears are on the same level.

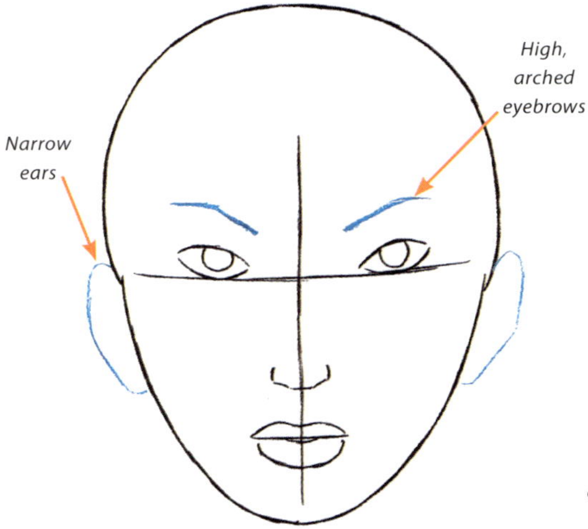

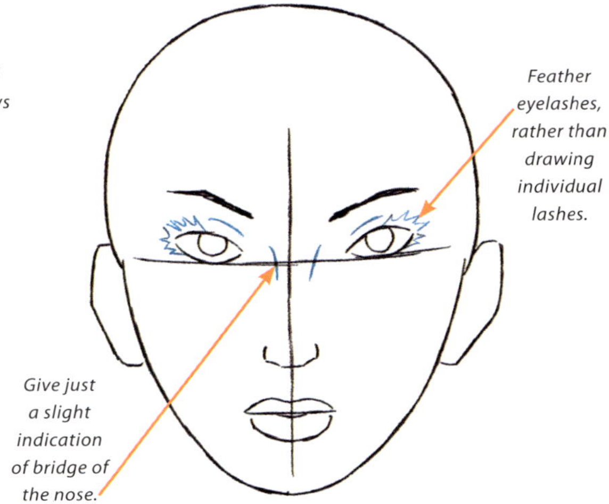

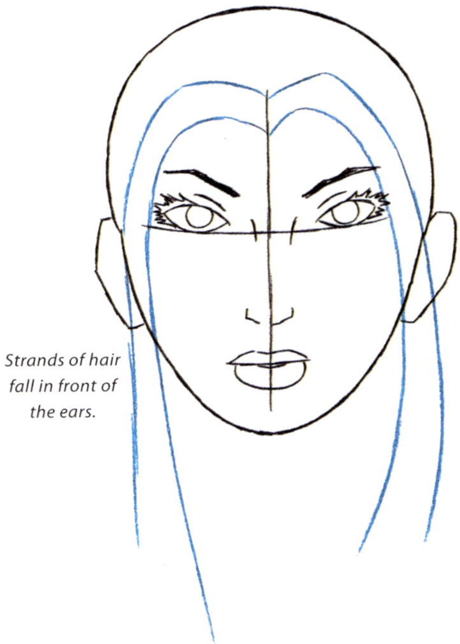

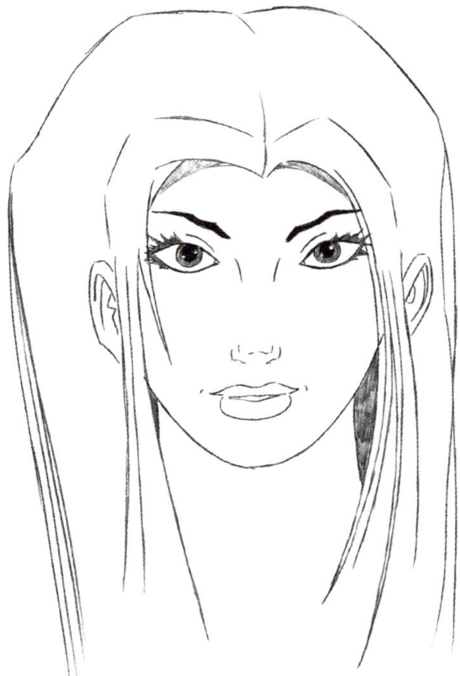

YOU TRY IT!

Use the basic head shape below as a guide to practice drawing the face with a cute hairstyle.

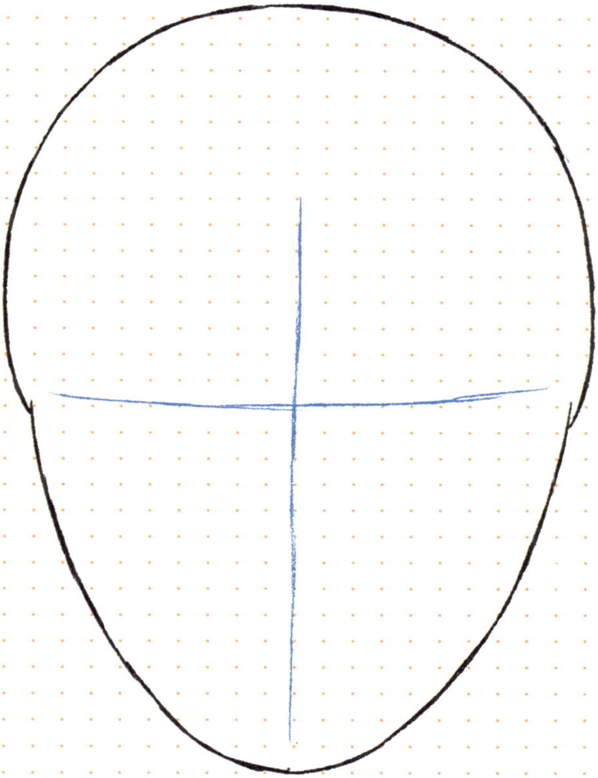

Hint

Guidelines help artists make sure that all the features line up correctly.

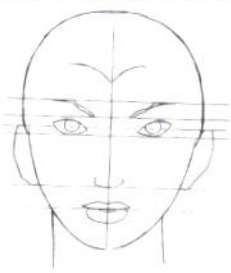

¾ VIEW—MALE FACE

As you turn the head to a ¾ position, the center line and the eye line remain as important as ever for placing the features of the face correctly on the head.

The male head is more angular than the female's, so it sometimes takes a little carving and tinkering to get its outline just right.

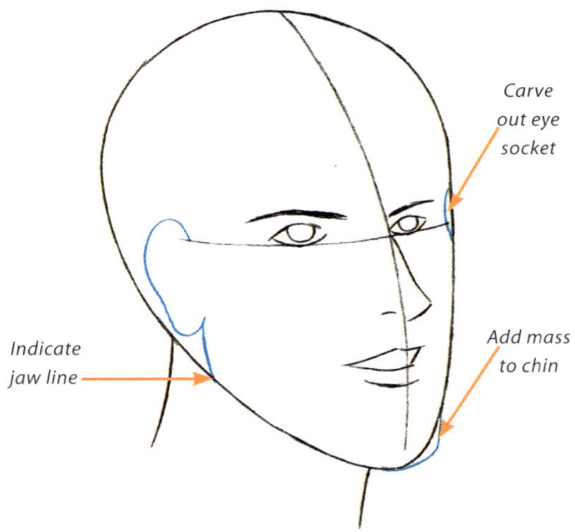

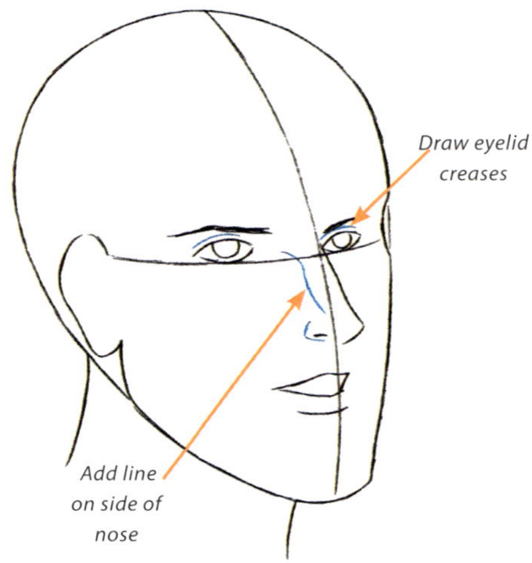

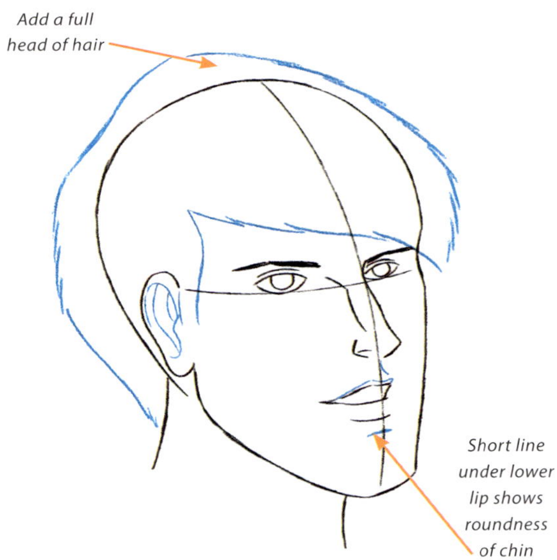

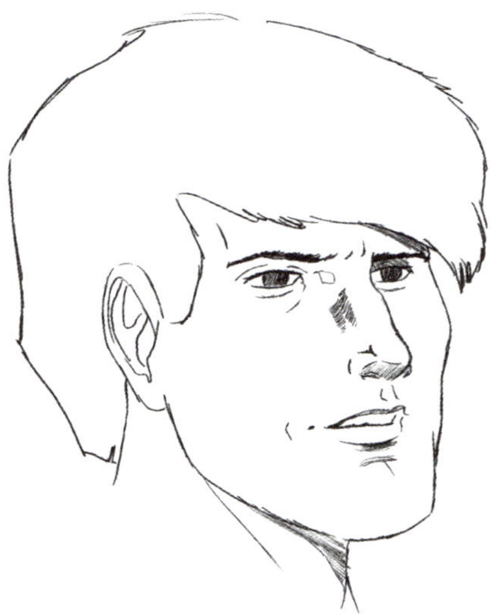

YOU TRY IT!

Use the basic head shape below as a guide to practice drawing the male face in ¾ view. (Focus on the eye placement.)

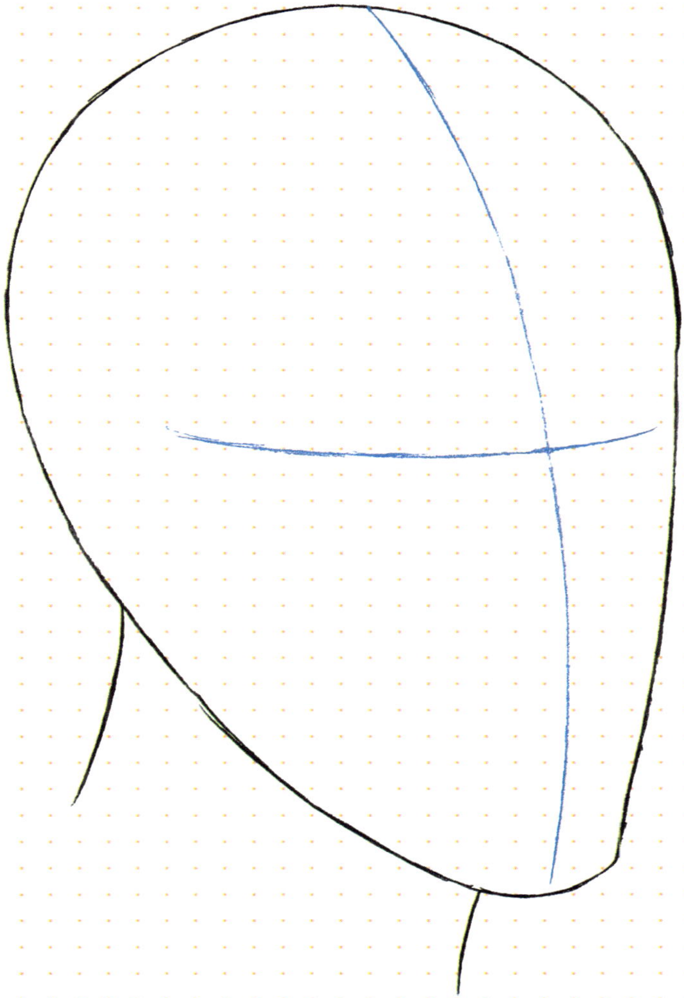

¾ VIEW—FEMALE FACE

To contrast the difference between drawing male and female heads, the more angular male ¾ view we just completed took several modifications to the basic head shape. However, this ¾ view of a female head starts as an egg shape and remains an egg shape throughout all of the steps.

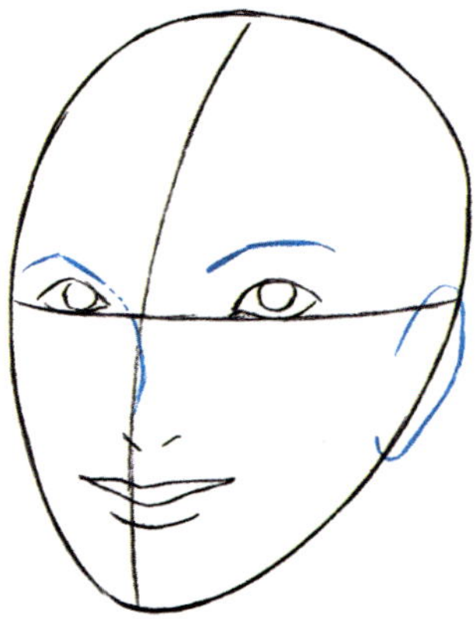

Drape the hair partially over one eye for a dramatic look.

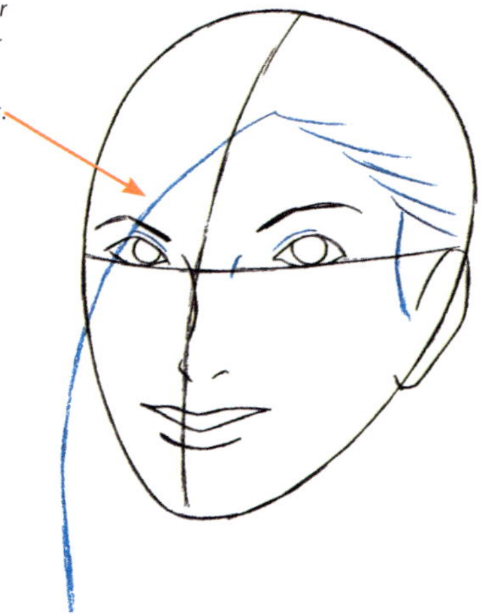

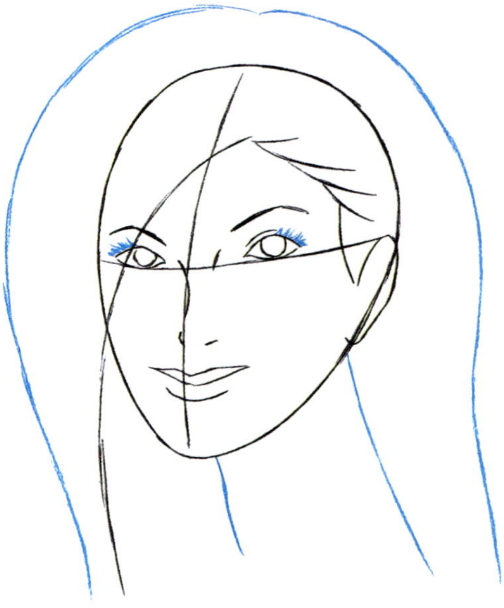

Fill out the hair.

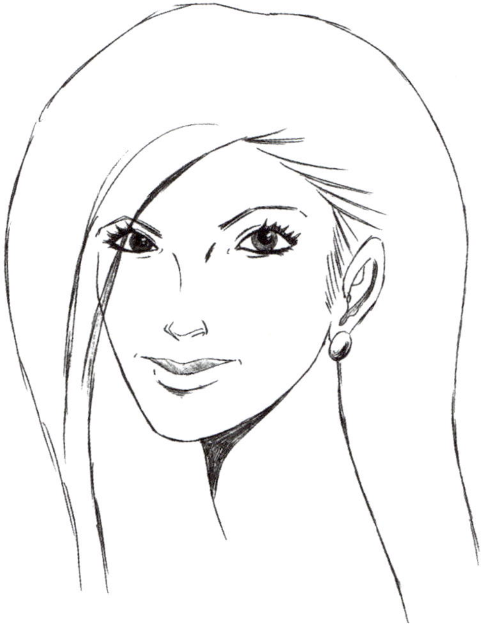

You can hide the eyes underneath the hair. However, you can also show the eyes in full, especially since we think of light hair as sort of translucent anyway. If the character has heavy bangs or very dark hair, this technique may not work as well.

YOU TRY IT!

Use the basic head shape below as a guide to practice drawing the female face in ¾ view.

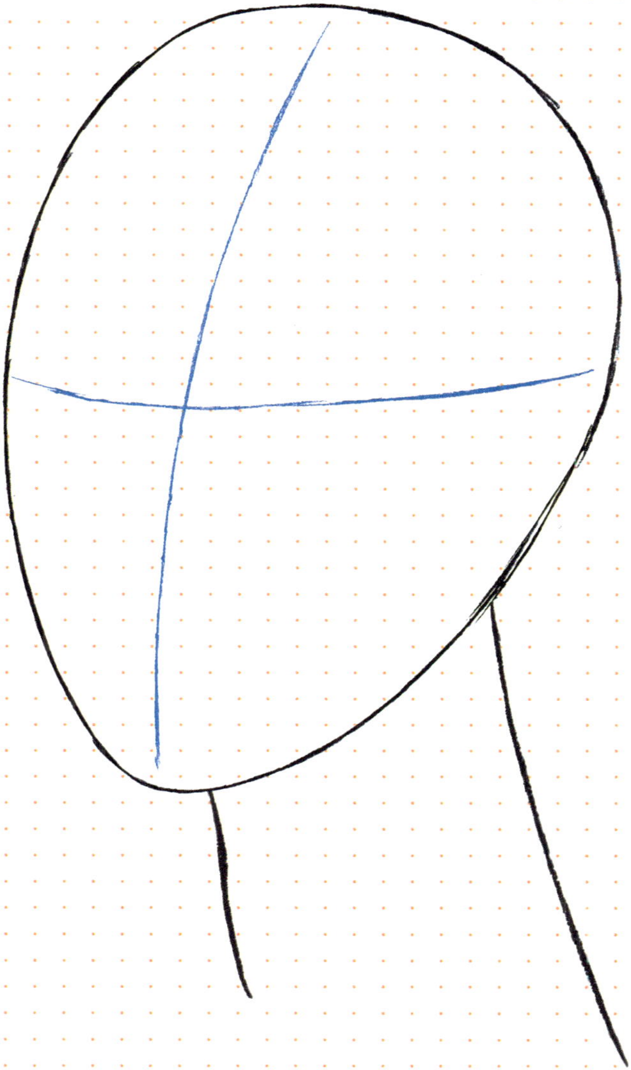

PROFILE—MALE FACE

Of all the angles of the head, the profile is probably the one that differs most between men and women. This male profile sports a protruding brow that hangs over the bridge of the nose as well as a protruding chin. His nose is straight, without the hint of a sweep. His eyebrow is close to his eye, with little arch. And his lips are thin.

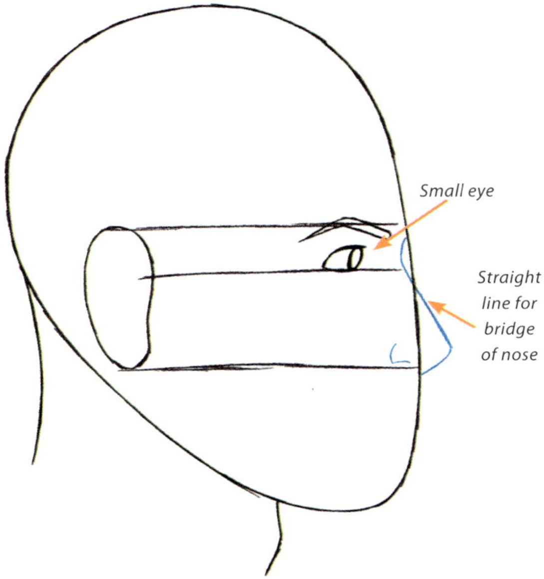

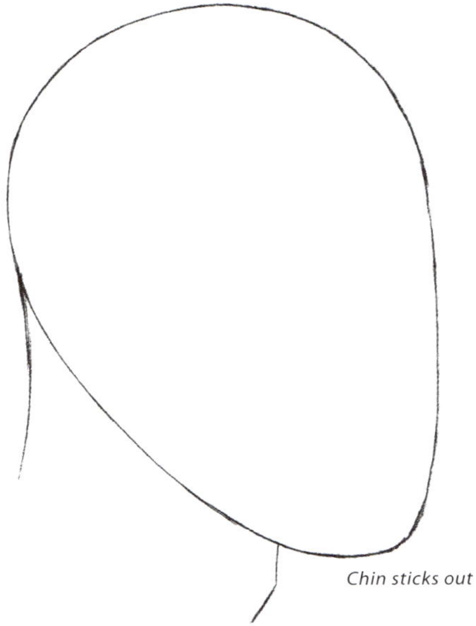

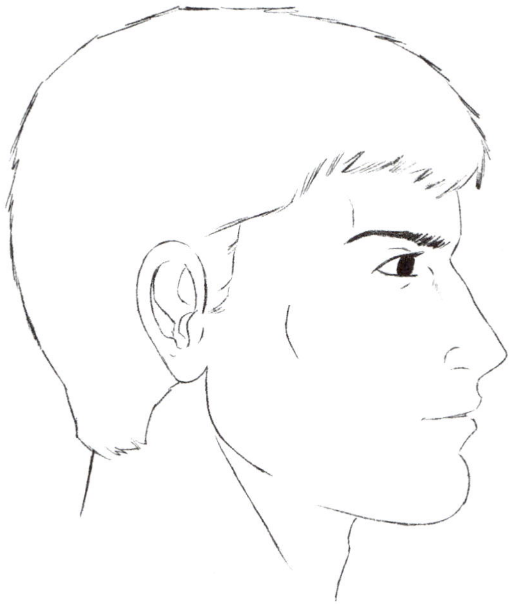

YOU TRY IT!

Use the basic head shape below as a guide to practice drawing the male face in profile. The upper guidelines bracket the eyes. The lowest guideline represents the bottom of the nose.

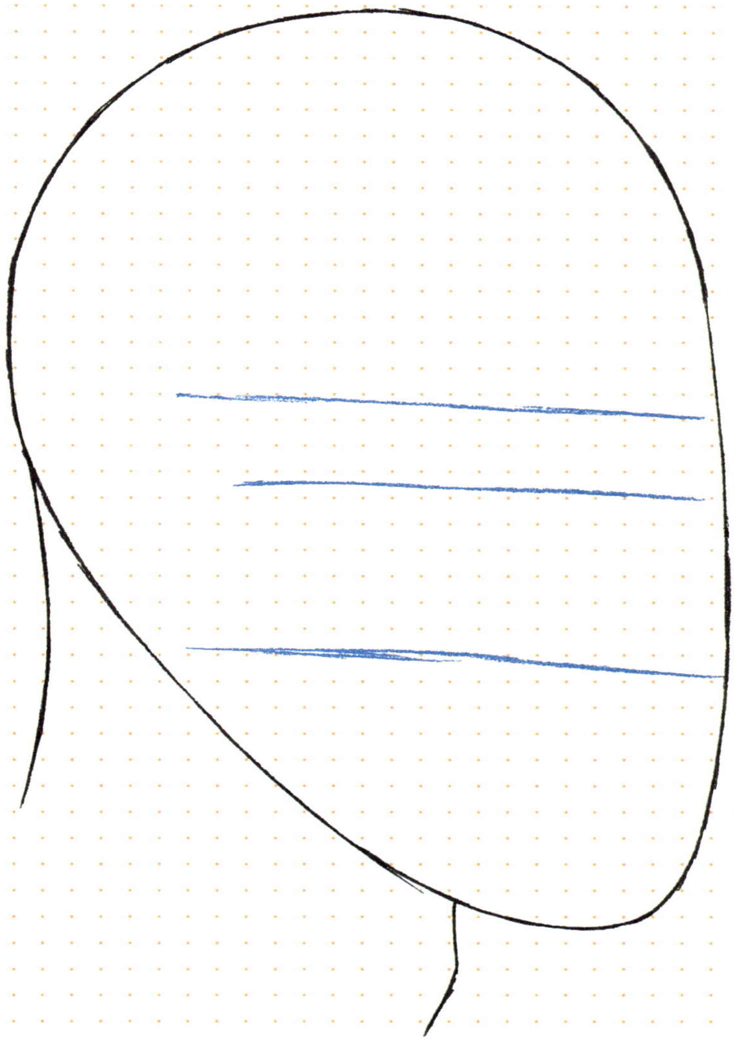

PROFILE—FEMALE FACE

For the female profile, soften the angles of the features as they shift direction in the profile. They should blend together, not bump up against one another abruptly.

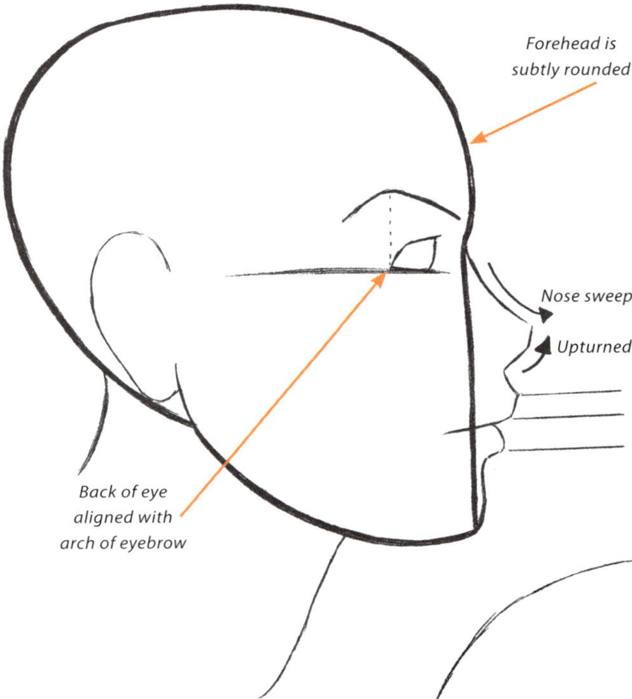

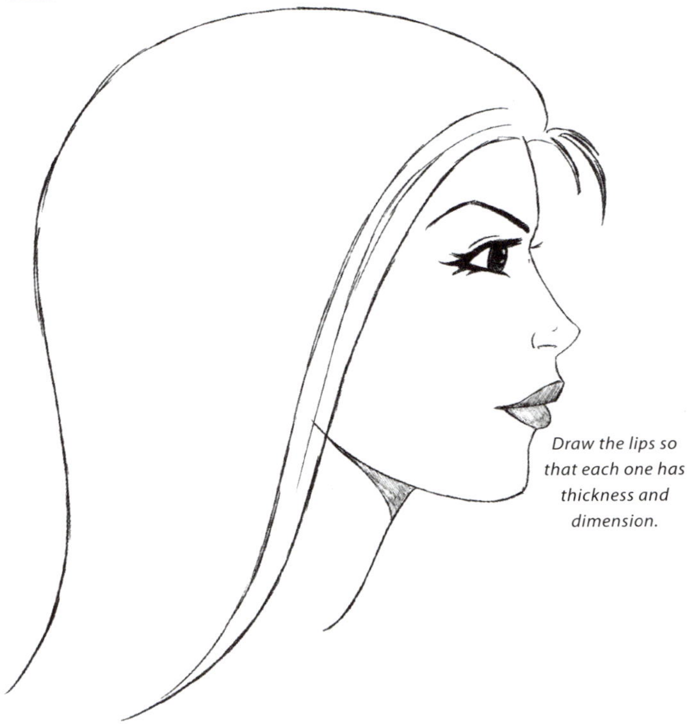

YOU TRY IT!

For the female profile, soften the angles of the features as they shift direction in the profile. They should blend together, not bump up against one another abruptly.

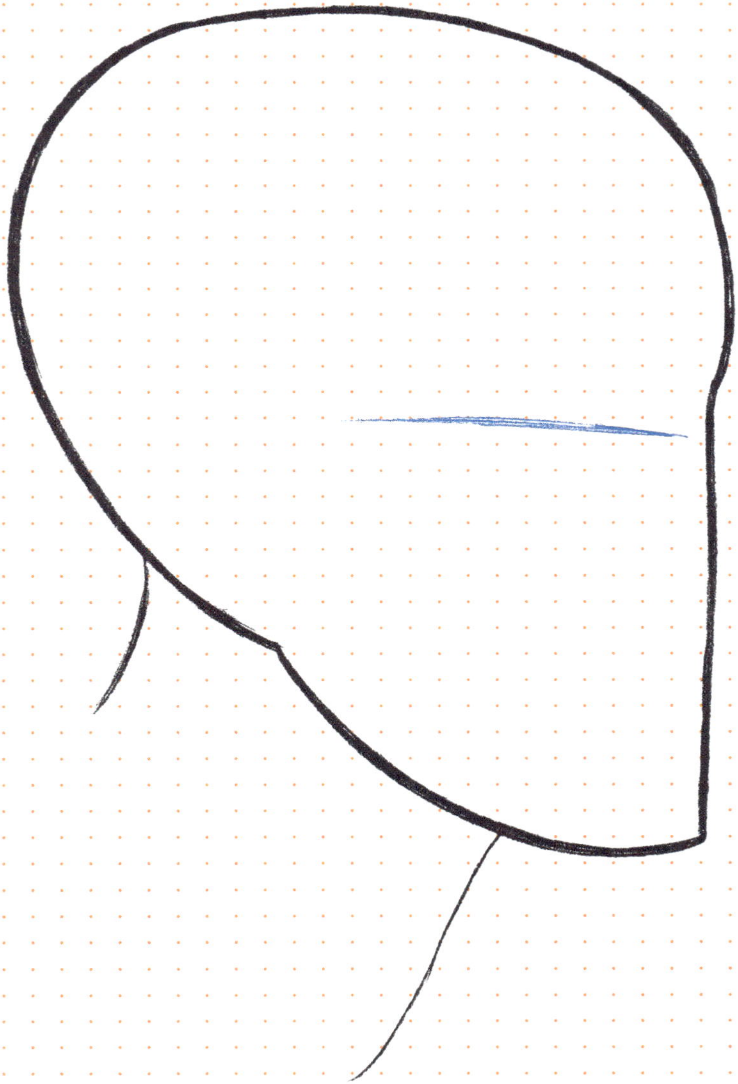

DRAWING THE BODY

DRAWING THE RIB CAGE

At its most basic, the rib cage can be drawn as just a hollow oval. This is a similar technique to using the egg shape as the foundation for drawing the head. And just like the head, we have to be able to turn the rib cage at different angles as the body turns. In these examples, I've sculpted the bottom of the rib cage and indicated its interior, but you don't have to. A simple oval is all that's required.

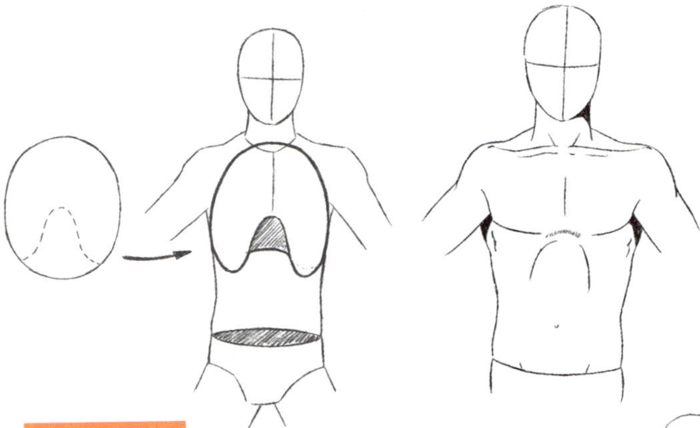

Front View

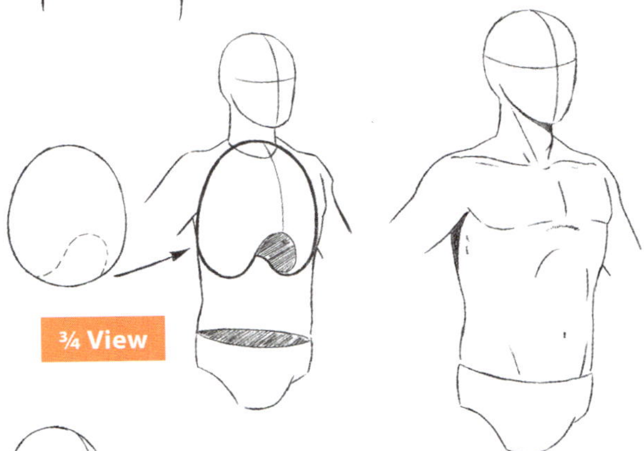

¾ View

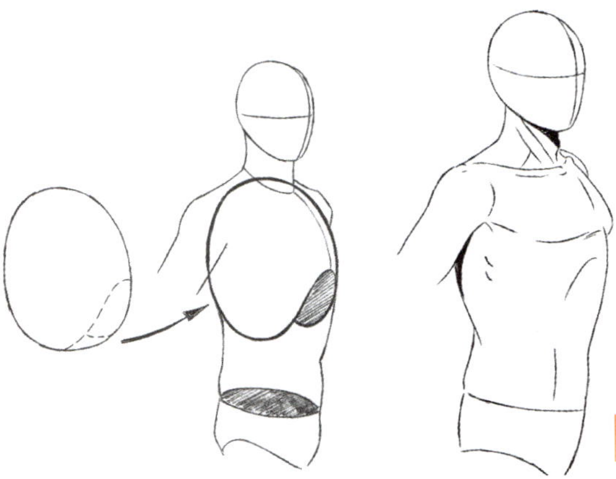

Side View

The side view on this page is actually not a true side view, because a bit of the body peeks out. This makes the drawing more dynamic.

YOU TRY IT!

Practice drawing the basic rib cage and torso construction from different angles in the space below.

CONTRACTING AND STRETCHING THE TORSO

The obvious way to avoid drawing a stiff figure is to put a bend in the body. Add a bend at the waistline on one side. On the other side, stretch the torso. The contrast between the two sides of the torso creates the appealing look.

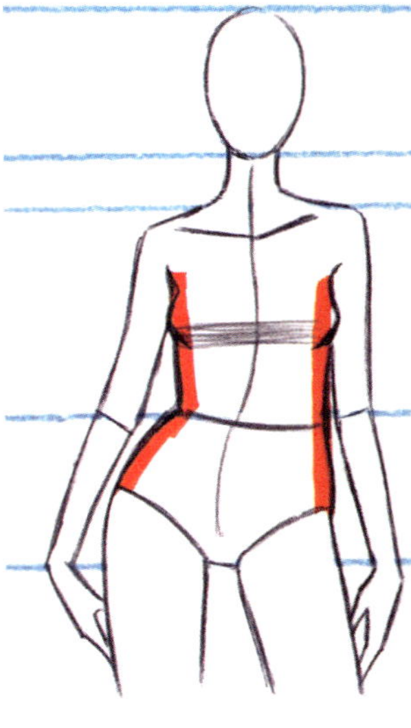

Torso contracts left, stretches right

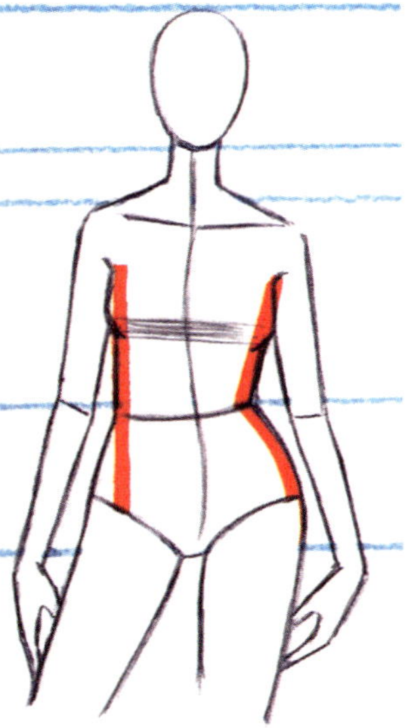

Torso contracts right, stretches left

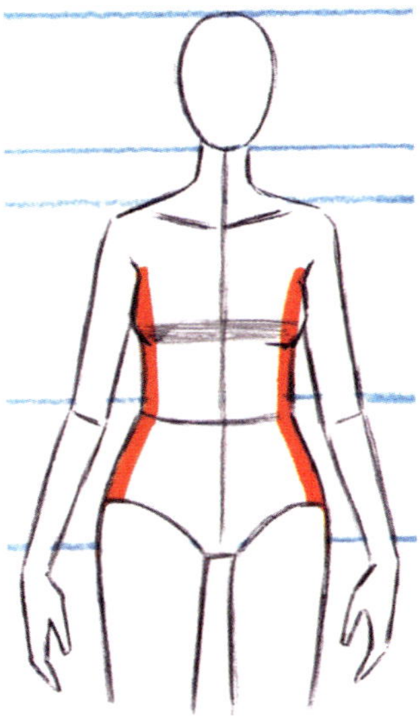

Static pose—torso is relaxed on both sides

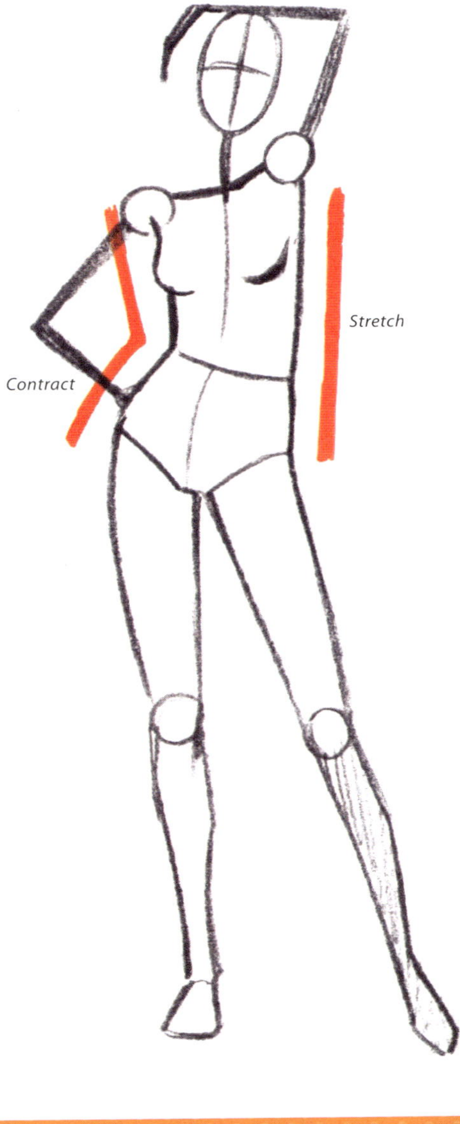

YOU TRY IT!

Use the guidelines below to practice drawing the torso in positions that contract and stretch.

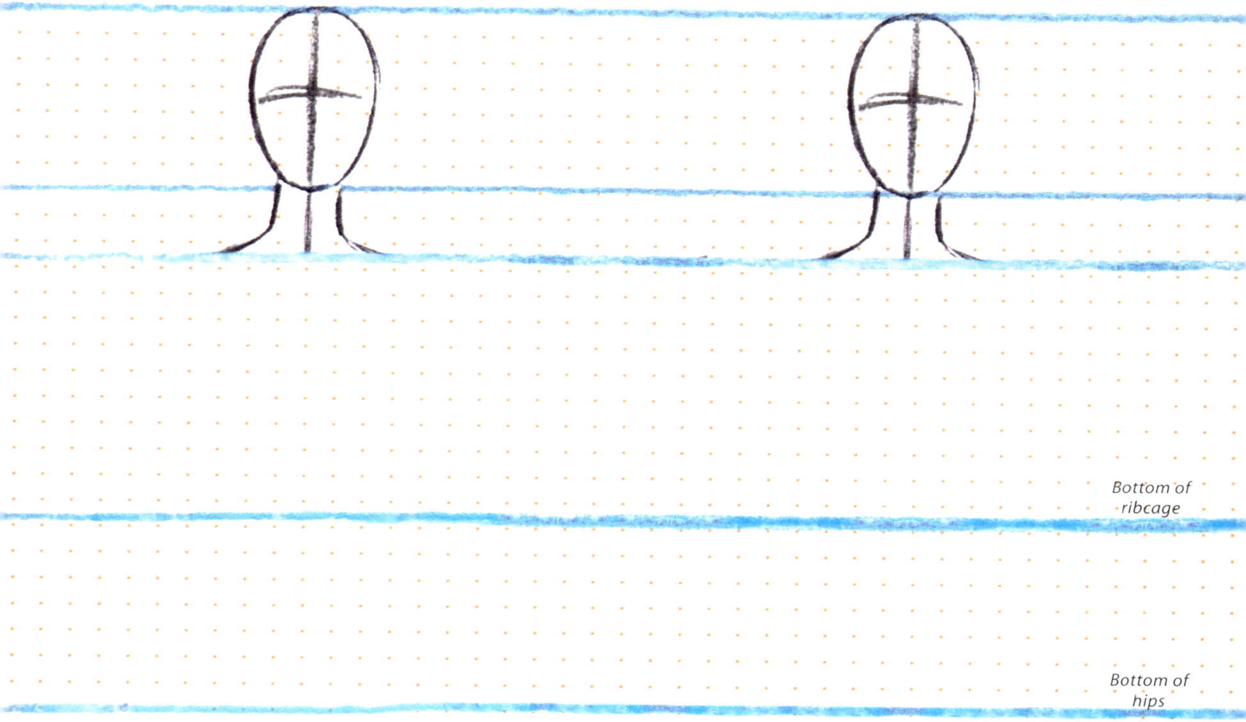

PROPORTIONS FOR ARMS AND LEGS: AN OVERVIEW

The arms and legs obviously extend from the torso, but how can you know how to draw them with the proper proportions? The following rule will enable you to add consistency to your drawing, removing the guesswork: The upper arms are longer than the forearms; likewise, the thighs are longer than the calves.

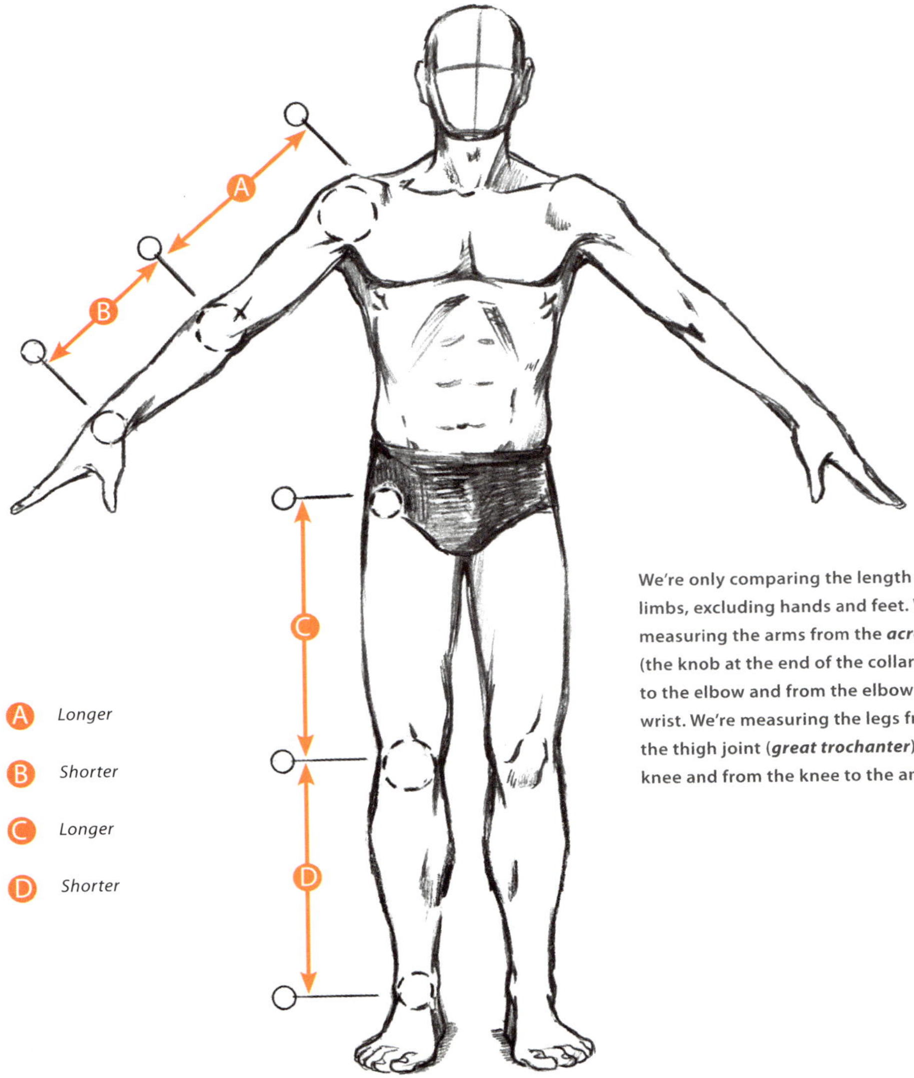

We're only comparing the length of the limbs, excluding hands and feet. We're measuring the arms from the ***acromion*** (the knob at the end of the collarbone) to the elbow and from the elbow to the wrist. We're measuring the legs from the thigh joint (***great trochanter***) to the knee and from the knee to the ankle.*

*For more instruction on body proportions, please see *Figure It Out: Human Proportions* by Christopher Hart.

YOU TRY IT!

Practice drawing the arm and leg proportionally on the right side of the body form below.

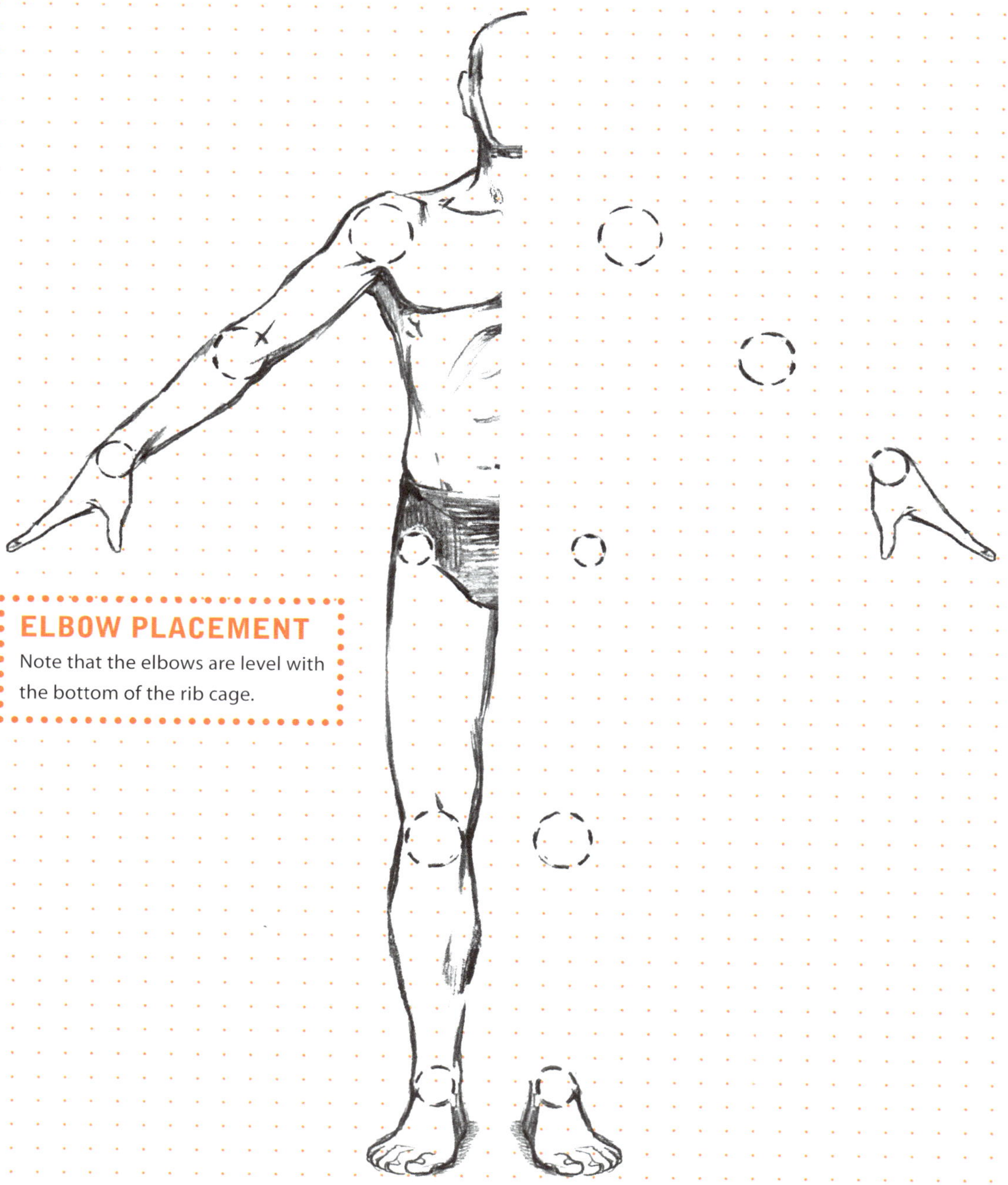

ELBOW PLACEMENT

Note that the elbows are level with the bottom of the rib cage.

WHAT TO DO WHEN THE ARM IS BENT

Now we know how to check proportions when the figure's arms are straight, but people don't carry themselves that way all the time. So how do you arrive at the correct proportions when the arm is bent?

It's not that complicated. Here's how to do it: Draw a vertical guideline where the arm would be if it were hanging straight down at the side of the body. Place marks at the shoulder joint (A); at the bottom of the rib cage, where the elbow would be (B); and at the pubic bone or crotch—the halfway point of the body—where the wrist would fall (C). Then measure the distance between A and B and between B and C, and simply apply those measurements to the arms in whatever position you choose to pose them.

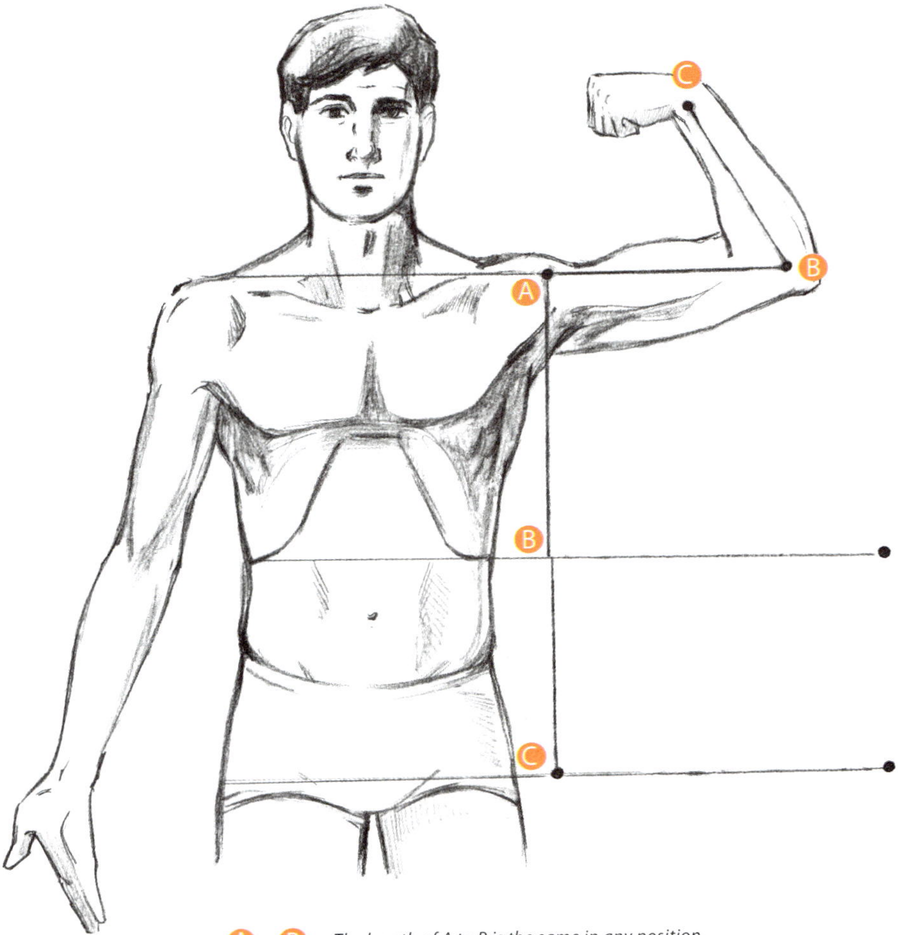

A B *The length of A to B is the same in any position (except when foreshortening is used).*

B C *The length of B to C is the same in any position (except when foreshortening is used).*

YOU TRY IT!

Practice drawing the bent arm in proper proportion to the body in the space below.

THE WRIST

Where the wrist falls in relation to the body determines the overall length of the arms. Hands are trickier to use as a measuring point because the hand can bend back and forth, and so can the fingers, which make the length of the hand variable. Not so if your measuring point is the wrist.

The wrist falls at the level of the crotch. Since the crotch is the midway point of the body, we can say that the wrist, when relaxed and at the side, appears at the halfway point of the figure. Technically, the wrist falls ever so slightly below the crotch, but the difference is inconsequential. Therefore, the wrist/crotch mark has been adopted as the standard.

Further, when the hand is open and the arm is relaxed at the side, the fingertips reach halfway down the upper leg.

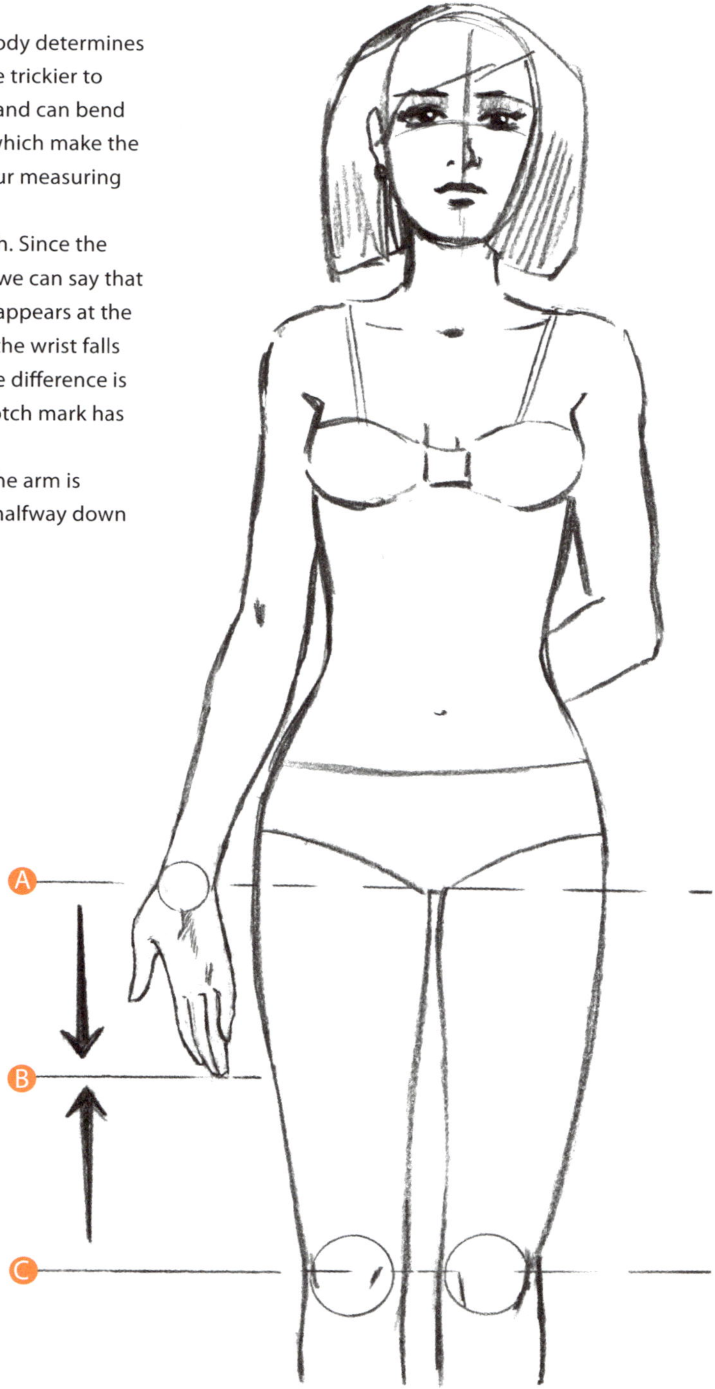

A *Level of crotch (or pubic bone)*

B *Midway point of thigh*

C *Knees*

YOU TRY IT!

Practice drawing the wrist in proper proportion to the arm and body in the space below.

DRAWING HANDS

Many people think that drawing hands is tricky. In your figure drawings, you won't always need to draw hands that are highly defined, but it is helpful to understand the basic proportions of how they are structured.

You can see that the middle finger is the longest, followed by the ring finger, the index finger, and the little finger. Therefore, the challenge lies in finding their relative size to one another. How much taller or shorter one finger is than another is not always so clear. The easiest way to determine this is to use the joints as measuring points. The index finger travels halfway up the first joint of the middle finger, for example. This diagram calls out more benchmarks.

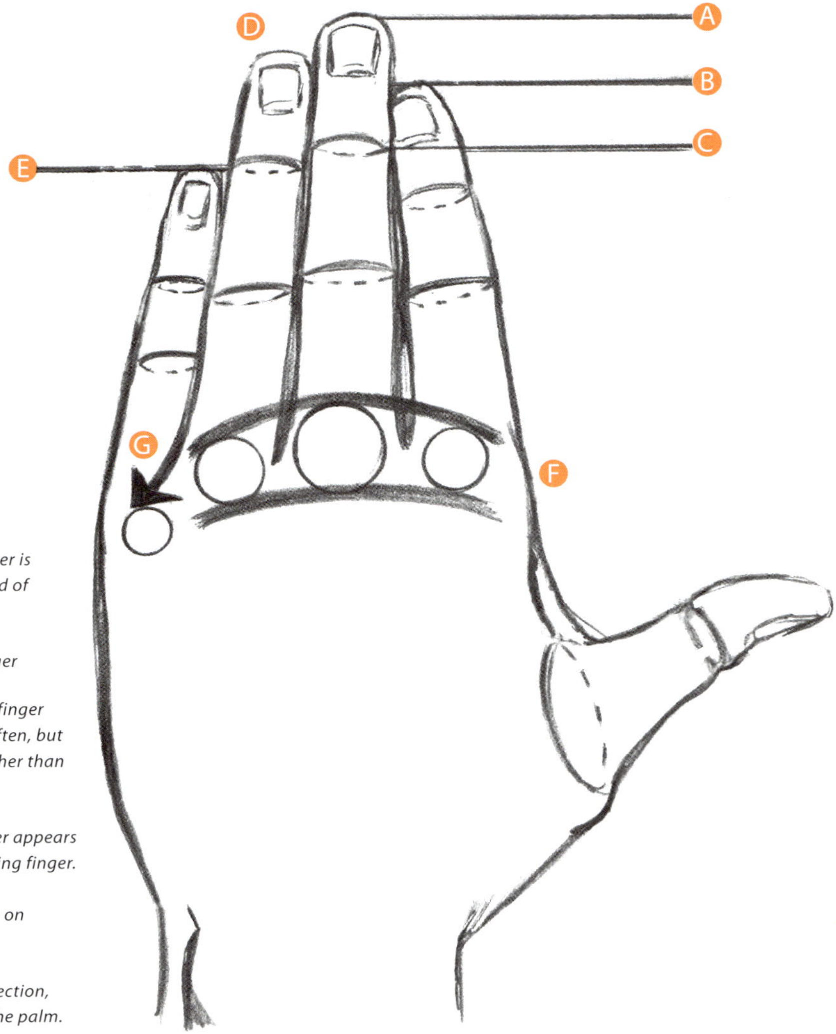

- A *Tip of middle finger*
- B *The tip of the index finger is halfway up the first third of the middle finger.*
- C *First joint of middle finger*
- D *A close look at the ring finger reveals that it is most often, but not always, a touch higher than the index finger.*
- E *The tip of the little finger appears at the first joint of the ring finger.*
- F *The knuckles are drawn on an arching guideline.*
- G *The skin tugs in this direction, toward the outside of the palm.*

YOU TRY IT!

Practice drawing a hand by following the proportion guidelines above. Once you've drawn the basic structure, try adding details for a more realistic look.

DRAWING FEET

Drawing feet at the correct size is as simple as using the head as a measurement. They're the same size. This illustration explains the concept. In practical use you would note, for example, that the length of the head is 2 inches long, so you would then sketch a foot that's also 2 inches long.

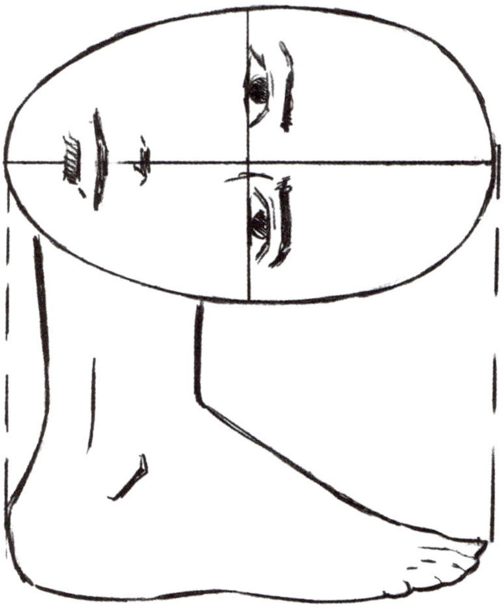

Equivalent length

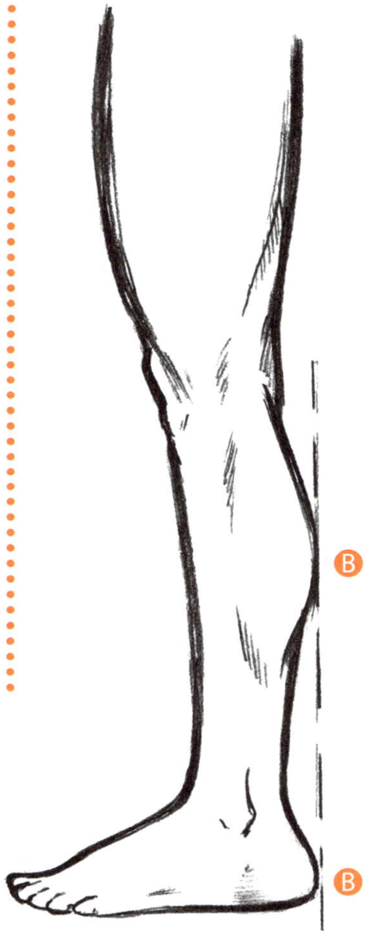

THE HEEL

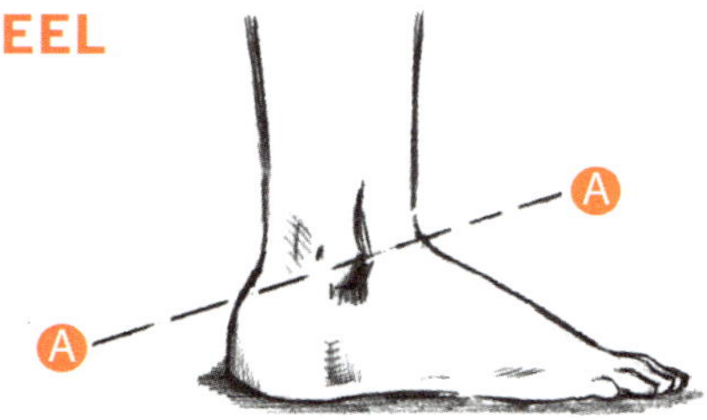

A The heel is lower than the instep.

B The back of the heel aligns with the widest part of the calf muscle.

YOU TRY IT!

Practice sketching feet in proportion based on the info above.

THE FRAMEWORK

Now let's put the basic components together to create a full, filled-out body. When drawing the basic figure, first sketch the overall form. Make a quick assessment, then make any revisions before you add and define the musculature. The muscles most used in basic figure drawing have been highlighted in red.

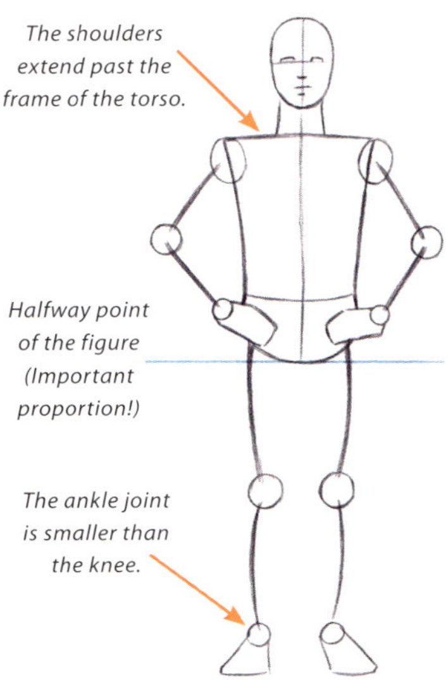

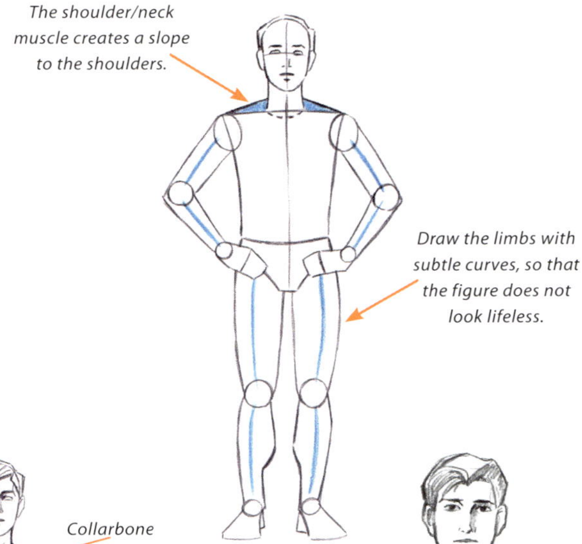

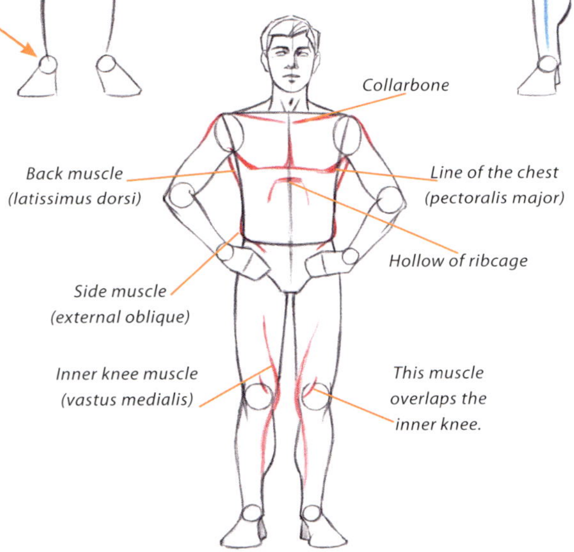

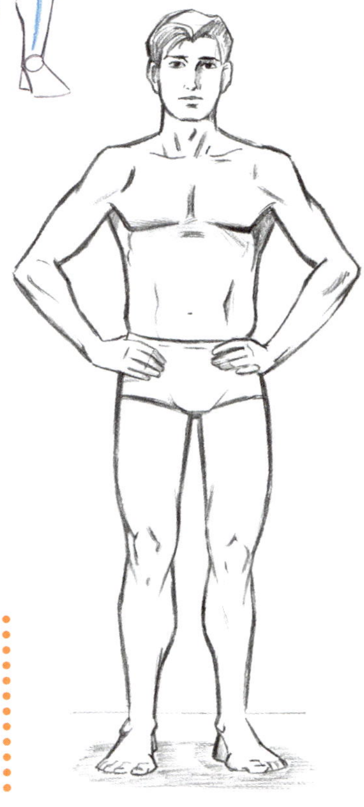

DRAWING THE MUSCLES

Even a well-posed figure needs some definition. This is done by suggesting the shape and location of the muscles, bones, and ligaments. And yes, this can also be suggested on clothed figures as well, as we will soon see.

YOU TRY IT!

Practice drawing the basic body form from the front view in the blank space below.

NECK REGION DETAIL

The neck and upper shoulders can be thought of as one section.

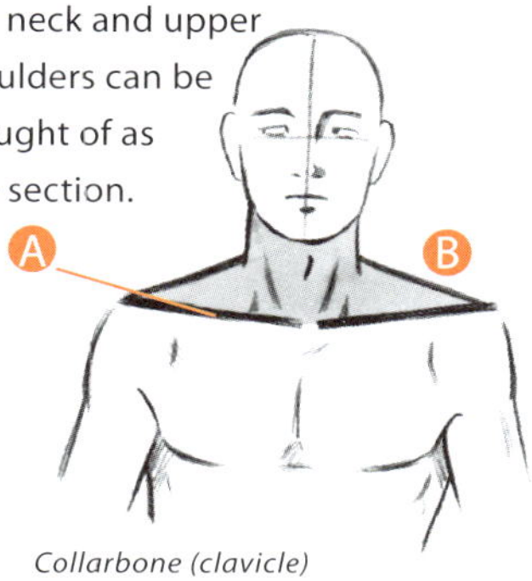

A *Collarbone (clavicle)*

B *Back muscles (trapezius)*

HIP DETAIL

Simplify the pelvis by drawing it as a bathing suit, which will emphasize its depth.

A *Draw the top of the hips to show depth (gray area)*

B *The holes for the legs are drawn on a diagonal.*

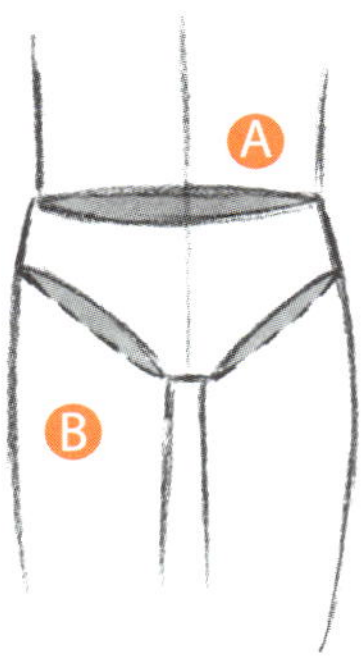

BACK VIEW

Because of its width, the back view can be a powerful-looking pose. When the shoulder blades are spaced well apart, a broad look is emphasized. Unless it is flexed or heavily muscled, the back is generally less articulated than the front of the torso. In this example, we'll add a slight bend to the waist for added practice.

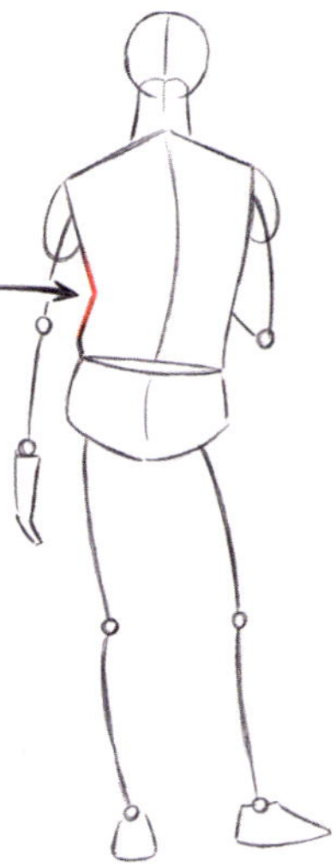

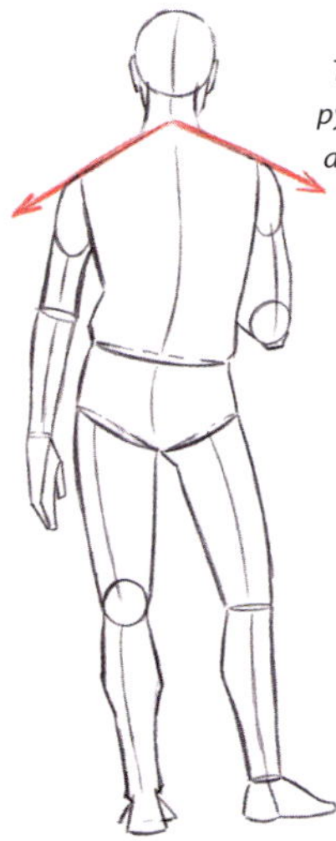

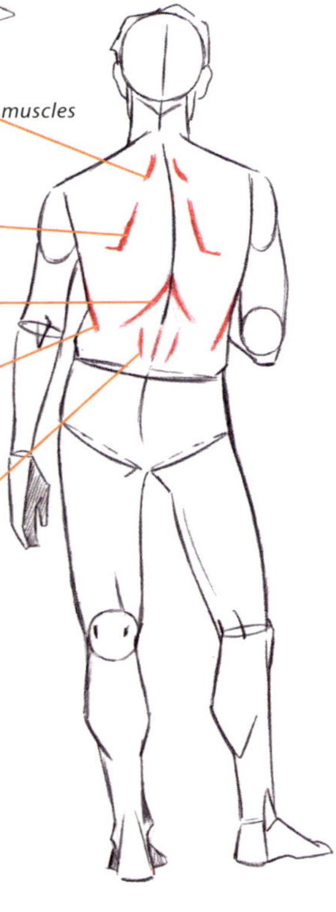

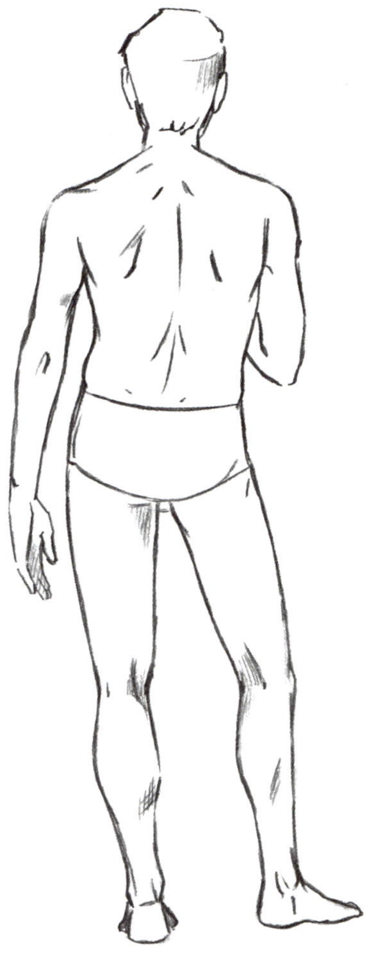

YOU TRY IT!

Practice drawing the basic body form from the back view in the blank space below.

Blank pages for freehand sketching

BODY DYNAMICS AND POSTURE

You'd think it would be easy to draw an ordinary standing pose, but there's actually a lot going on with the body that occurs when a person is simply standing still.

THE NATURAL WAY TO STAND

In order to portray someone standing up straight, you need to draw curves. Sounds wrong, but it's true. When standing, the rib cage and the hips naturally tilt at opposite angles from each other. This is what creates the look of the rounded tummy line and the curve at the small of the back.

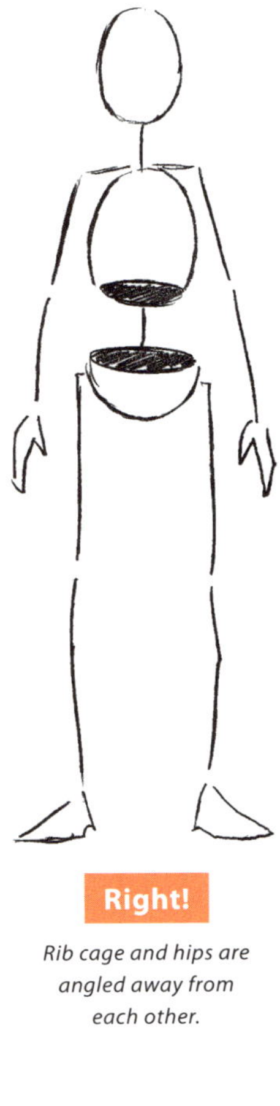

Right!

Rib cage and hips are angled away from each other.

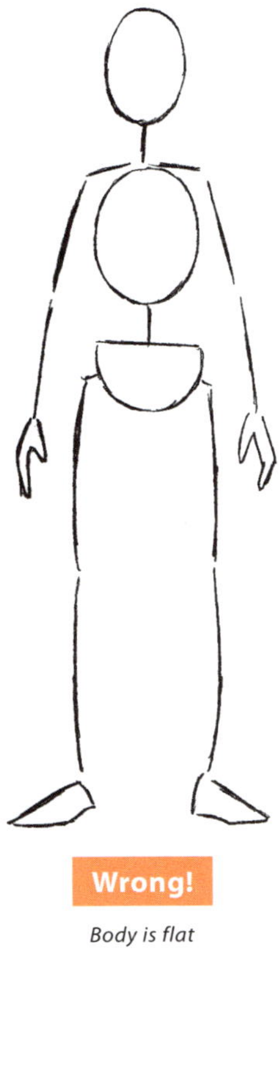

Wrong!

Body is flat

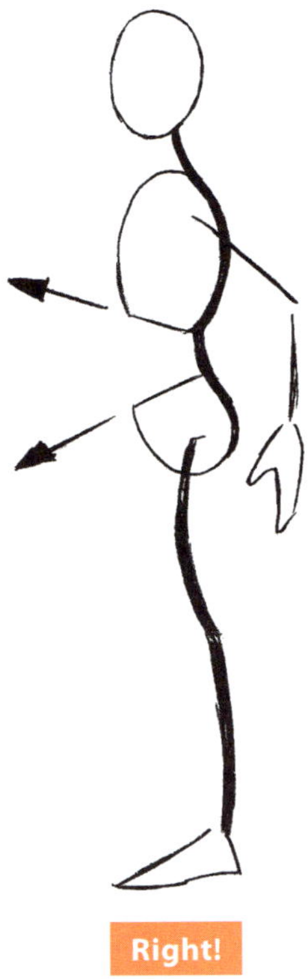

Right!

Spine is curved. The rib cage and hips are angled away from each other.

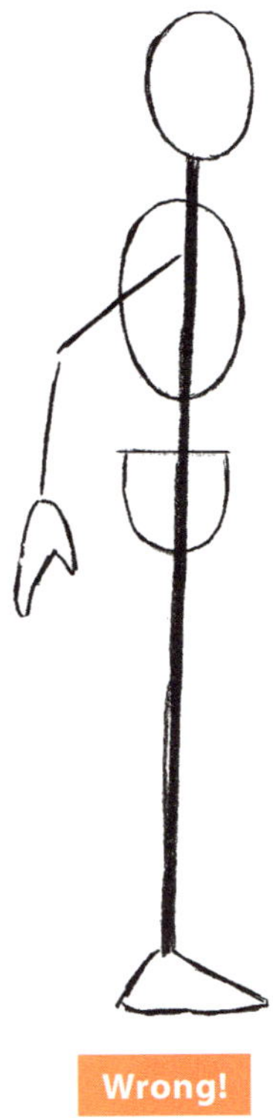

Wrong!

Spine is a straight line. The body is flat. So stiff, so rigid. So boring.

YOU TRY IT!

Practice drawing the basic body frame with natural curvature throughout.

BENDING

The spine, although far from being a rubber band, is much more malleable than many beginning artists realize. It gives the body great flexibility.

BACK AND FORTH

The spine can bend backward only to a limited degree (unless you're a contortionist!), but it can bend forward much farther with relative ease. Note the change in the angle of the hips as the body leans back and then bends forward.

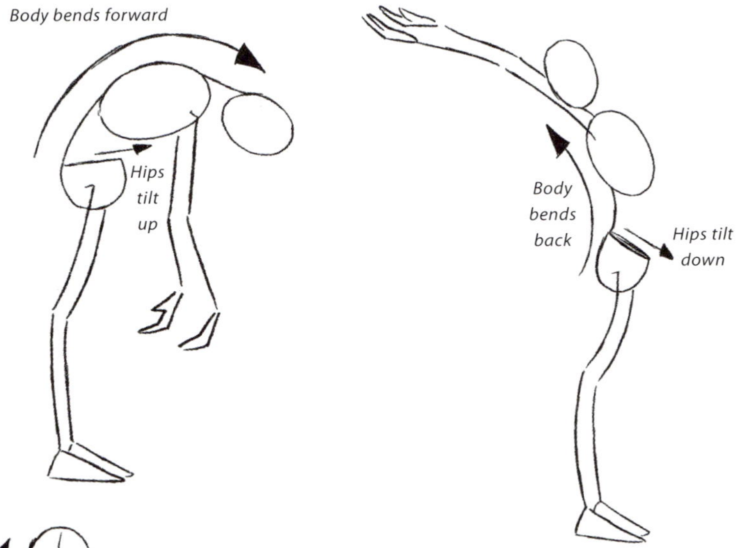

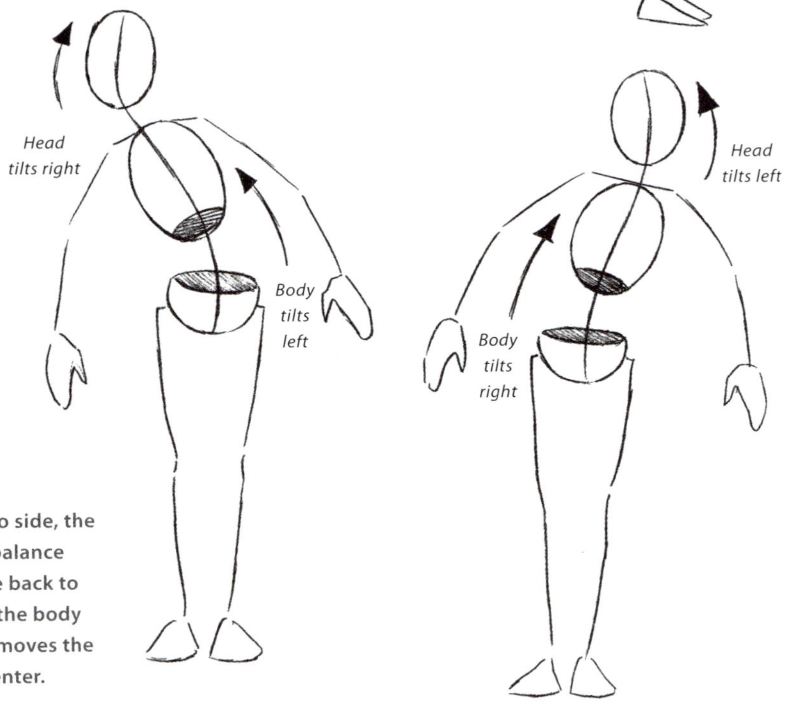

SIDE TO SIDE

When bending from side to side, the body will try to maintain balance by bringing the center line back to the starting point—i.e., if the body moves one way, the head moves the other to get back to the center.

YOU TRY IT!

Draw the basic figures above, paying attention to the natural curvature of the spine.

CURVE OF THE SPINE

Now we'll look at how body dynamics affect posture on some fully fleshed out figures. In these examples, the figures are fully clothed, but the body's basic musculature still determines how they are drawn.

STIFF POSE

Well, he's standing with straight posture all right. But he also looks like he'd tip over in a strong breeze. This is the approach you often see beginners take, because it's intuitive. But unfortunately, it doesn't work.

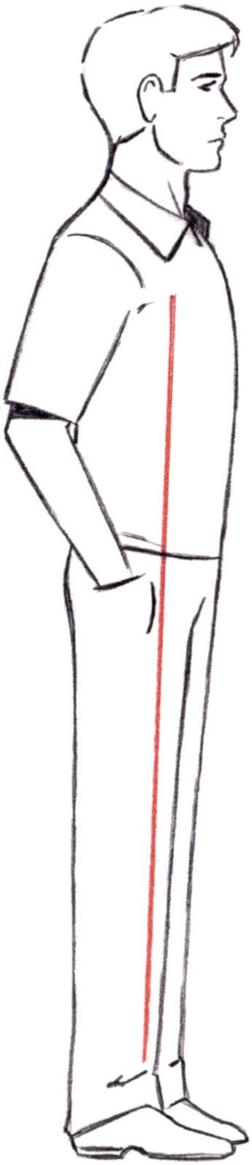

NATURAL POSE

There's counter-balancing going on here. As the torso curves outward, the legs curve inward, as represented by the Line of Action (red guideline). It's a small adjustment, but it makes a world of difference.

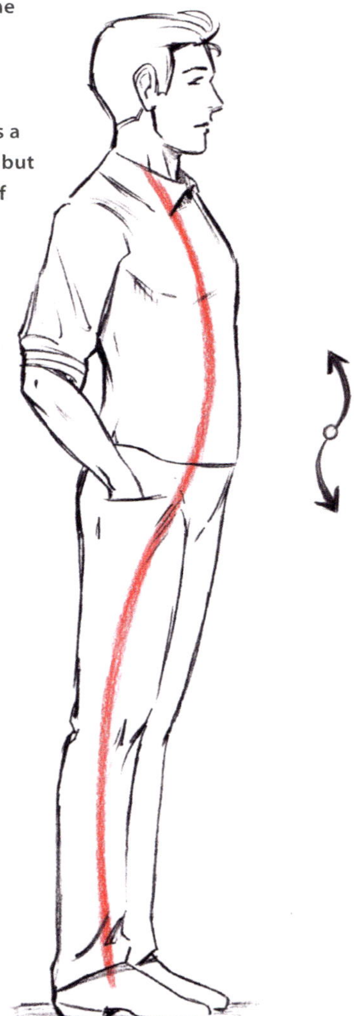

YOU TRY IT!

Practice drawing this classic, side-view posture with a fluid spine. Start by drawing the curved Line of Action first, then draw the figure around it. You can make this a rough sketch—we'll break it down step by step on the next page.

CLASSIC POSTURE (SIDE VIEW)

To the average viewer, this figure appears to be standing straight, but it's actually built on a series of curves.

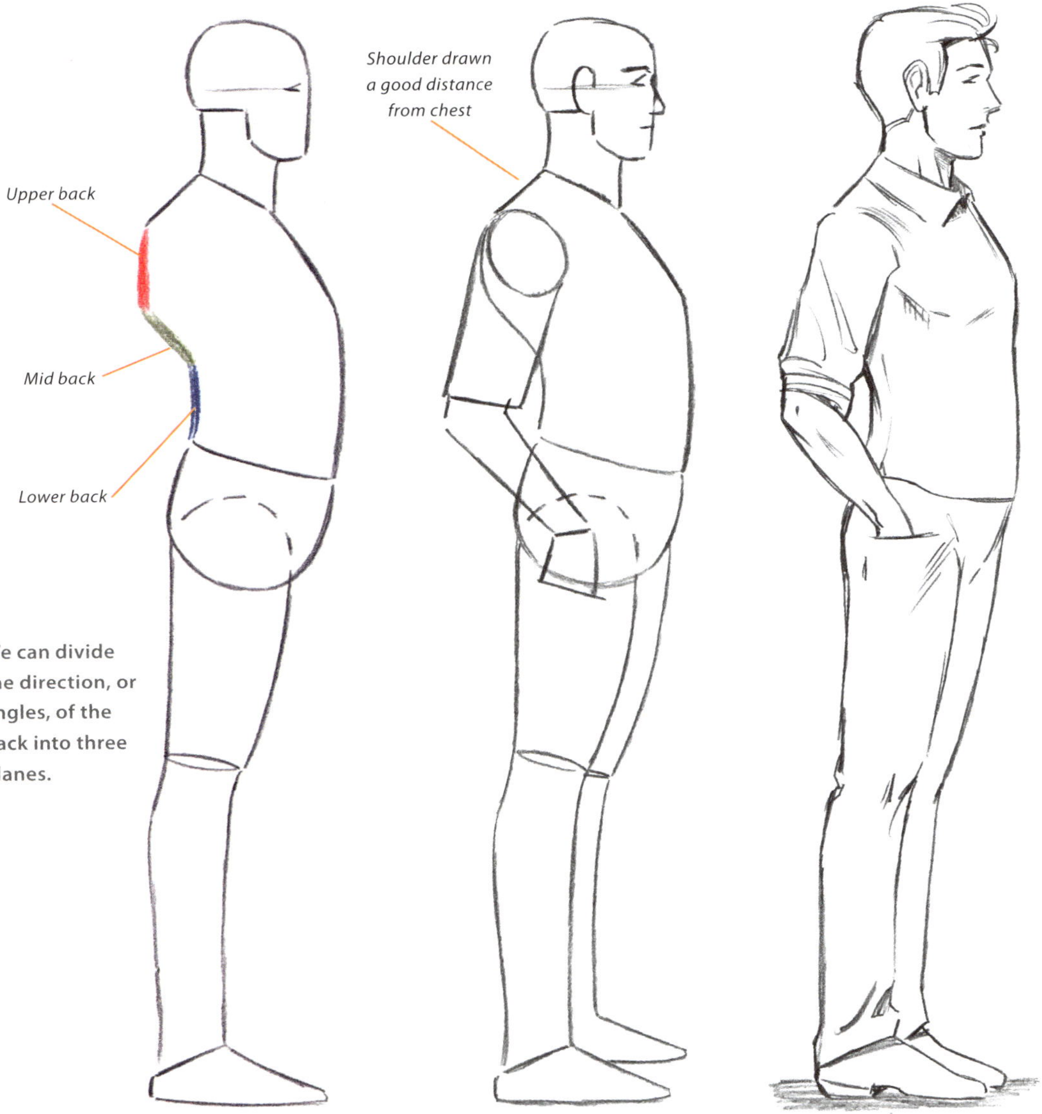

We can divide the direction, or angles, of the back into three planes.

POSE POINT

To look comfortable, the posture needs to show an overall flow.

YOU TRY IT!

Now you can refine the sketch you did on the previous page by drawing this classic side-view pose step by step.

HOW REAL PEOPLE STAND

The classic posture, outlined on the previous page, is the way you stand when your doctor measures your height. In real life, the body relaxes and settles. This causes the hips to move forward and the chest to sink. Let's try it.

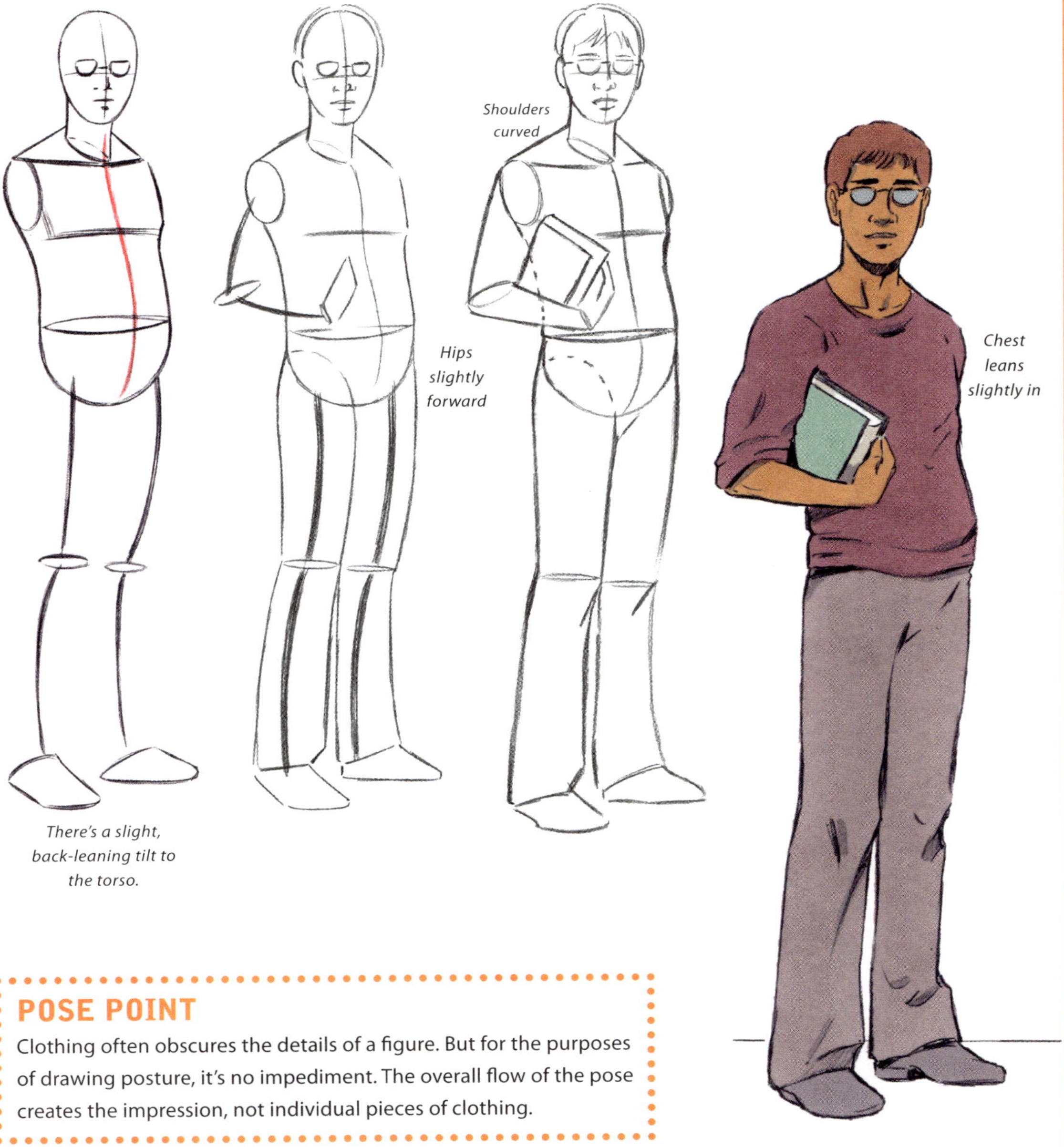

POSE POINT

Clothing often obscures the details of a figure. But for the purposes of drawing posture, it's no impediment. The overall flow of the pose creates the impression, not individual pieces of clothing.

YOU TRY IT!

Practice drawing this common body stance in the space below.

BACK VIEW (POSTURE)

When the body is relaxed, the pose looks natural. Create a flow between the upper and lower bodies so that they move as a flexible unit.

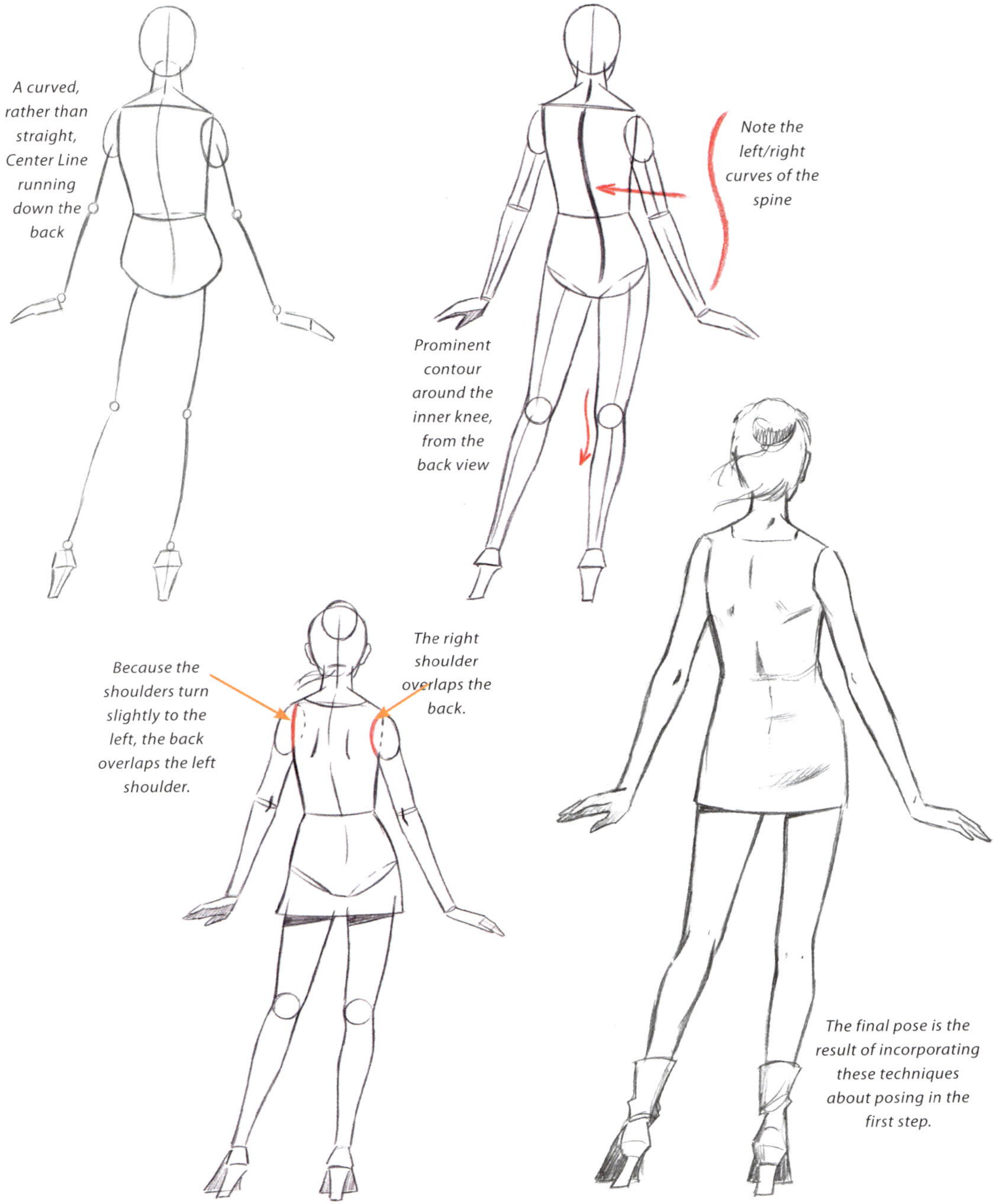

YOU TRY IT!

While practicing drawing the figure above, note how the Center Line dictates the position of the upper and lower body. Note how the hips shift slightly right, while the upper body shifts slightly left—just like the Center Line.

ARRANGING ARMS AND LEGS

This straight pose may not appear basic, but it is. Her posture is very straight, and her weight is distributed evenly without so much as a bend at the waist. The pose is completely symmetrical. So what gives it a dramatic look? The bold placement of the arms and legs. This placement on a basic straight figure acts as an introduction to drawing more complex poses.

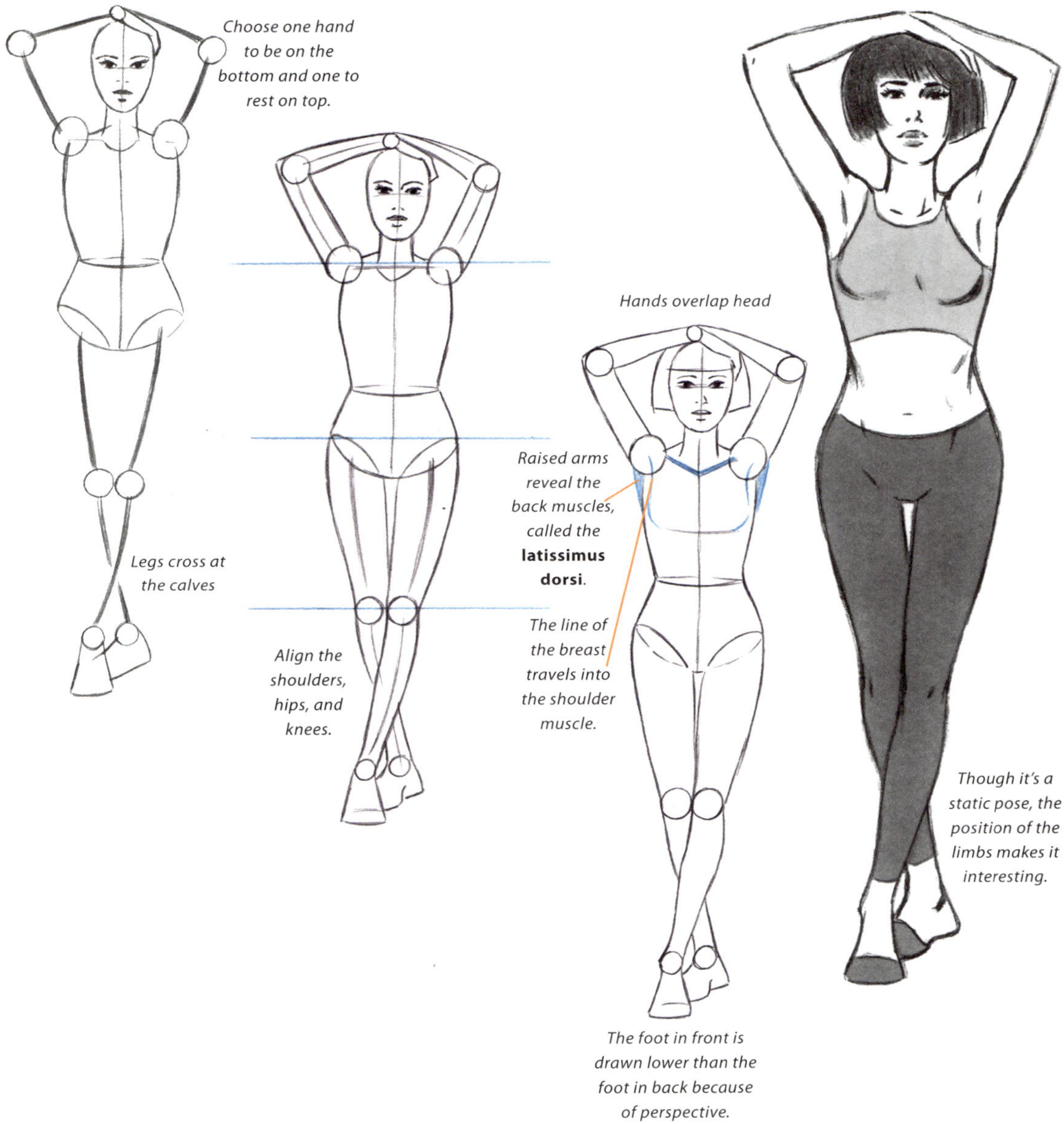

YOU TRY IT!

Use the blue proportion guidelines to keep this pose symmetrical.

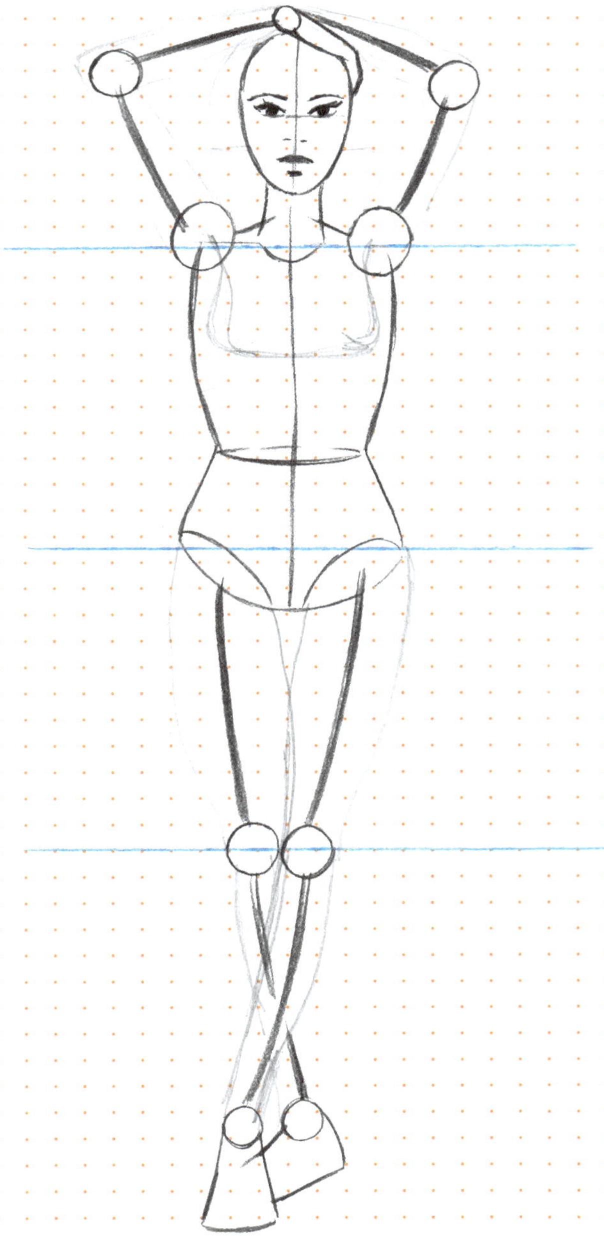

YOU TRY IT!

Now practice drawing the pose on the previous page without the guidelines.

CREATING VARIATIONS

You can create a variation on this pose easily by simply raising or lowering an arm. Use the guide below to easily create a new pose.

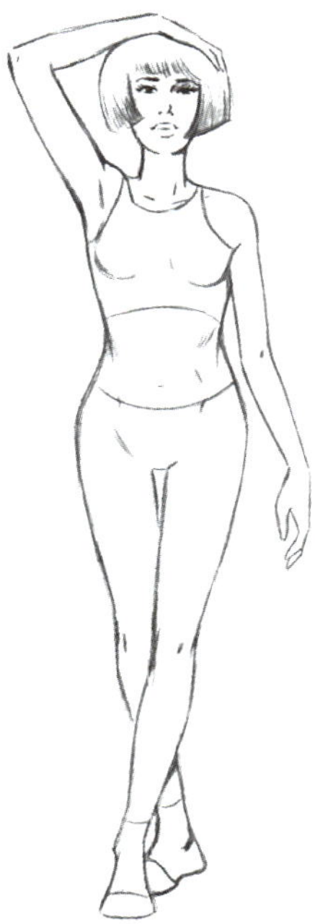

MORE PRACTICE WITH VARIATIONS

As we've just seen, changing the positions of the arms, legs, or both is an excellent way to create variations in poses. Another is to shift the weight slightly to one side or the other, bend a knee inward, or move a leg nearer or further from the body. Even a slight shift can create a more dramatic pose.

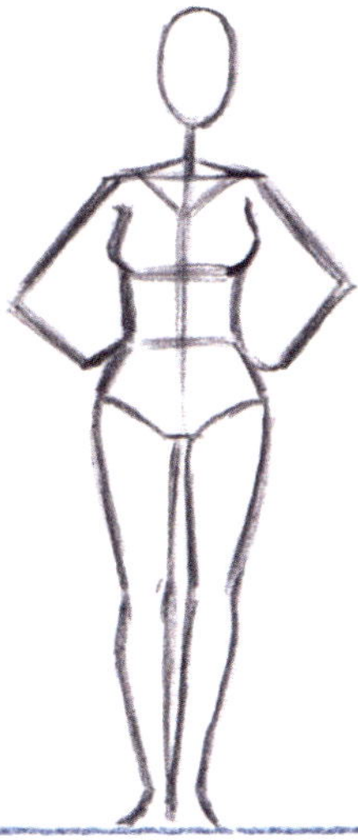

Static

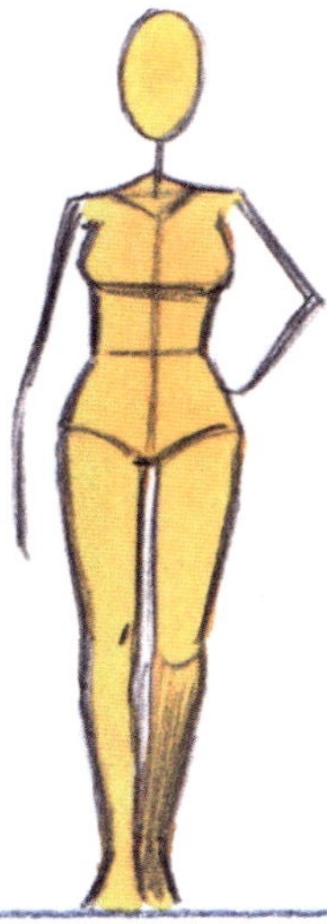

Variation: arm down, leg slightly bent

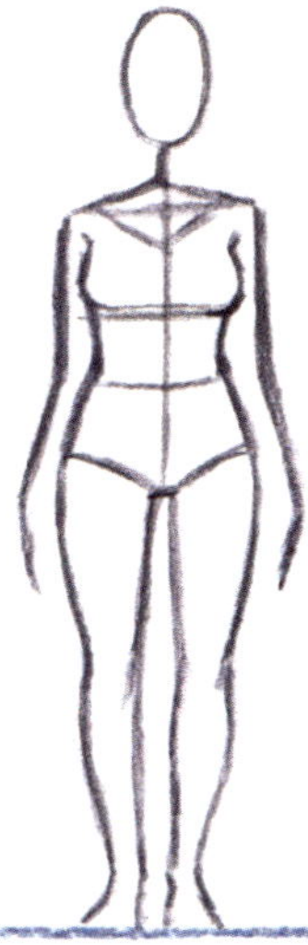

Static

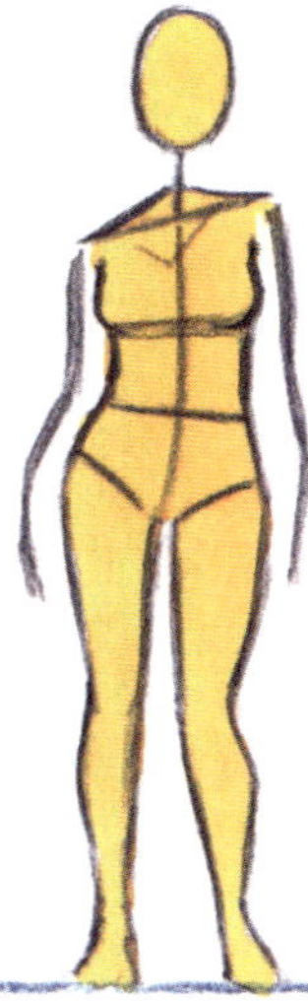

Variation: shoulder dips and leg bends inward

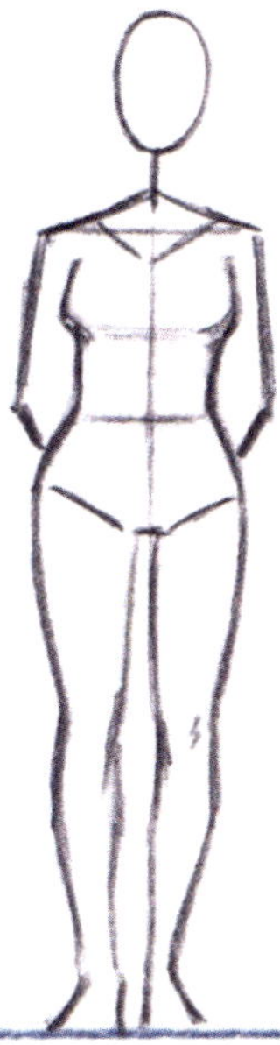

Static

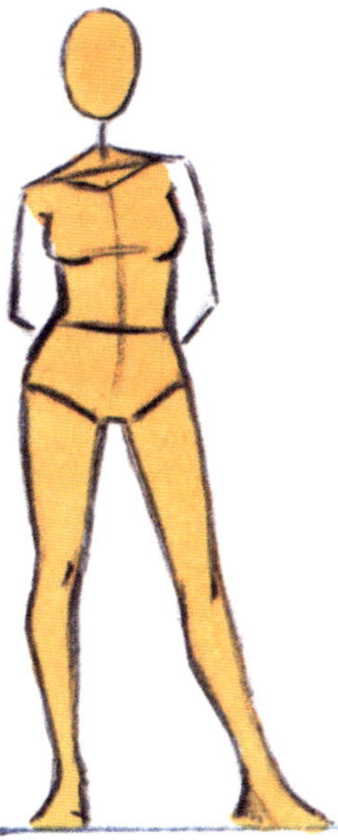

Variation: leg away

YOU TRY IT!

Practice drawing variations on a basic, straight-standing figure in the space below.

BODY LANGUAGE

Earlier, we drew various facial expressions: pleased, worried, surprised, skeptical, etc. Now we're going to communicate a variety of attitudes through body language alone. This exercise in drawing basic body forms will help propel us into the upcoming chapters, where we will draw more defined men and women in many different poses.

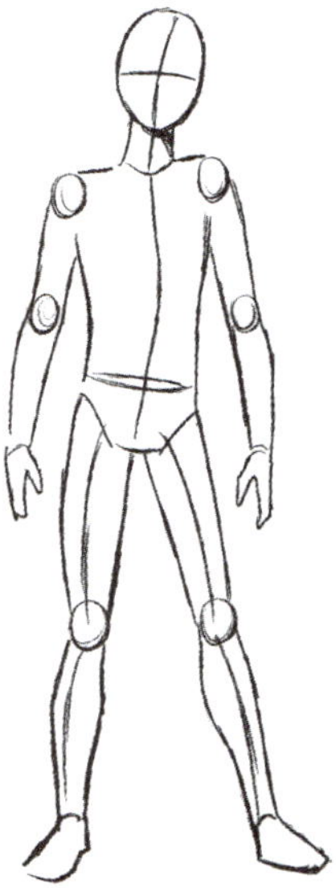

Confident

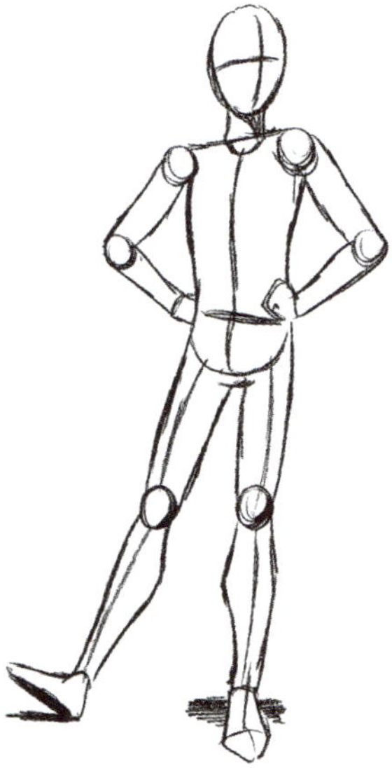

Impatient

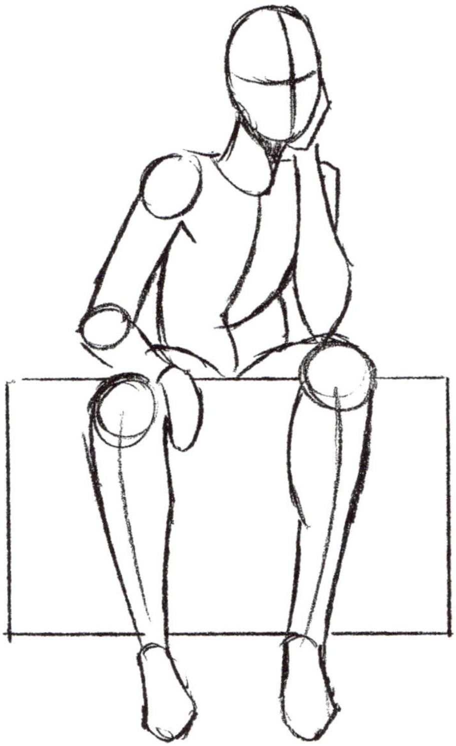

Waiting

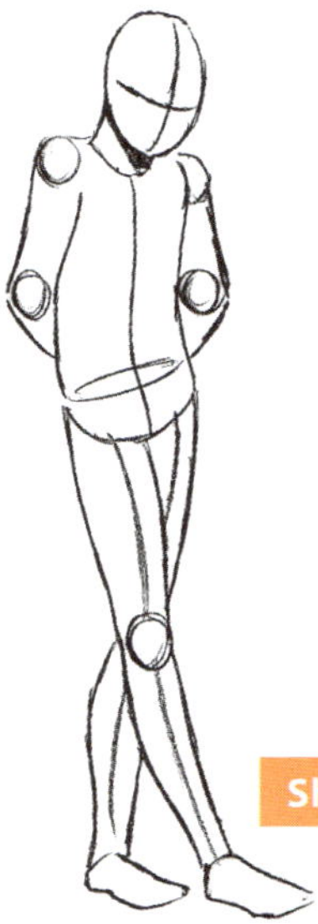

Shy

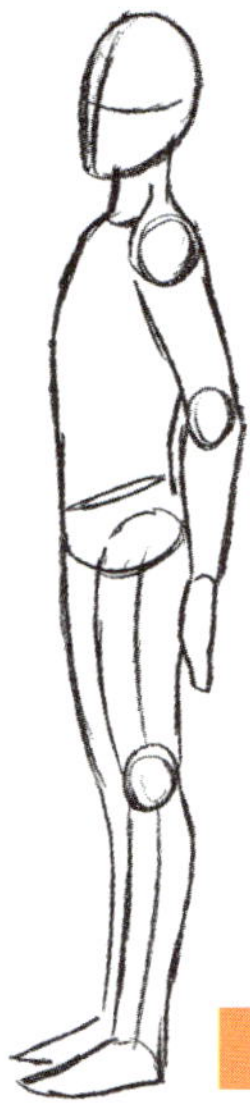

Alert

YOU TRY IT!

Practice sketching the body language in these poses in preparation for drawing more complex poses.

MORE BODY LANGUAGE PRACTICE

Note how shading creates body planes in side and ¾ views.

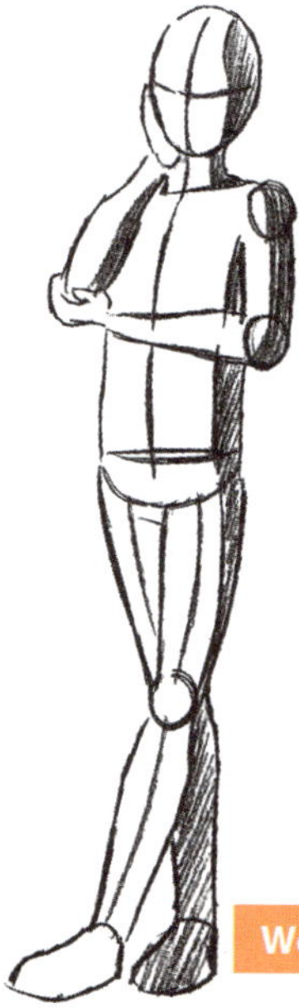

Wondering

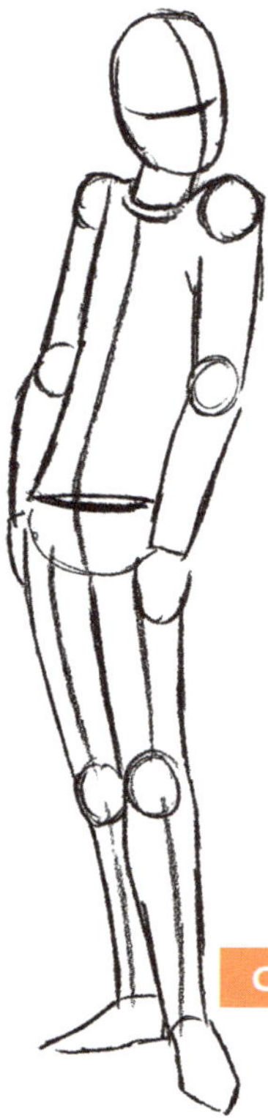

Curious

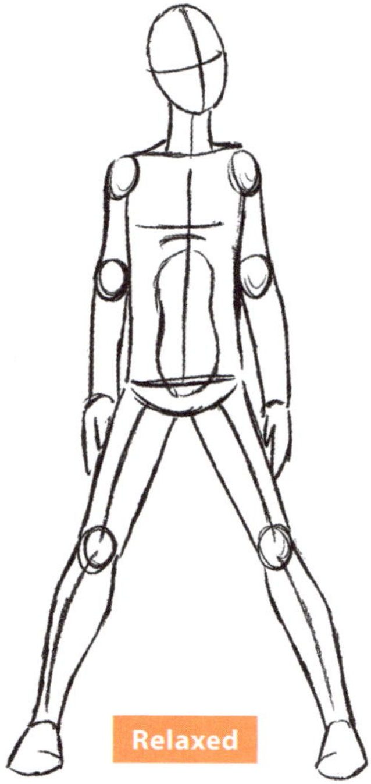

Relaxed

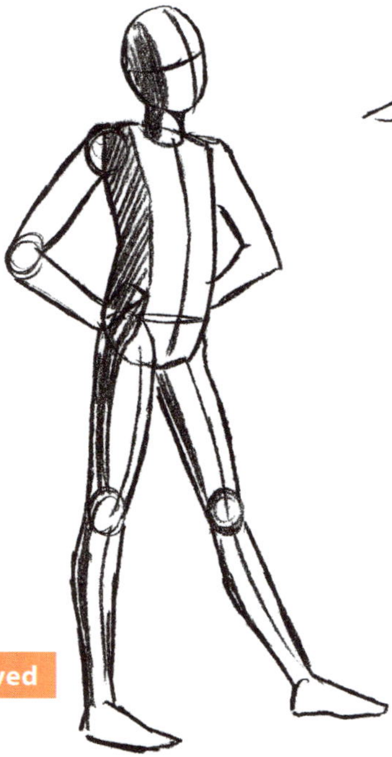

Annoyed

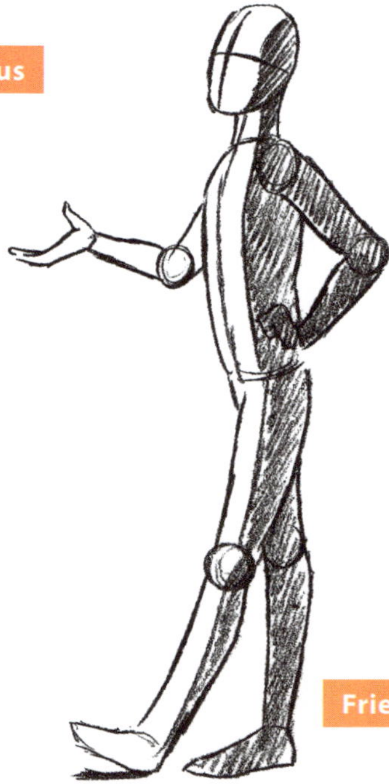

Friendly

Blank pages for freehand sketching

DRAWING WOMEN

We now move on to the next phase in our ever-advancing pursuit of artistic skills: full-fledged figure drawing in more complex poses. First, we'll cover female figures.

BALLET POSE

Posture is everything when drawing a ballerina, so take special note of the angles of the back. Fully extend the arms and legs to accentuate their length.

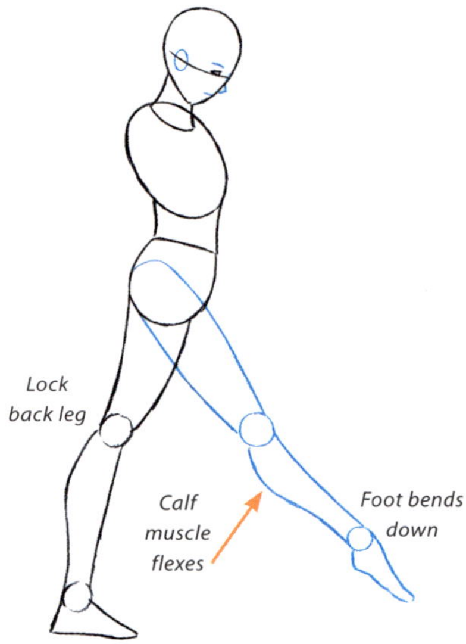

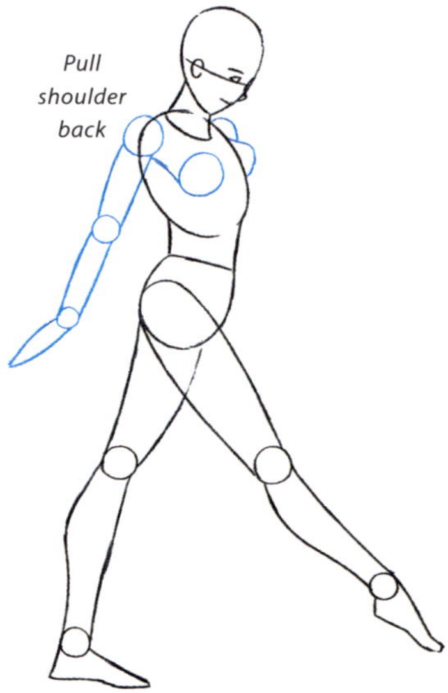

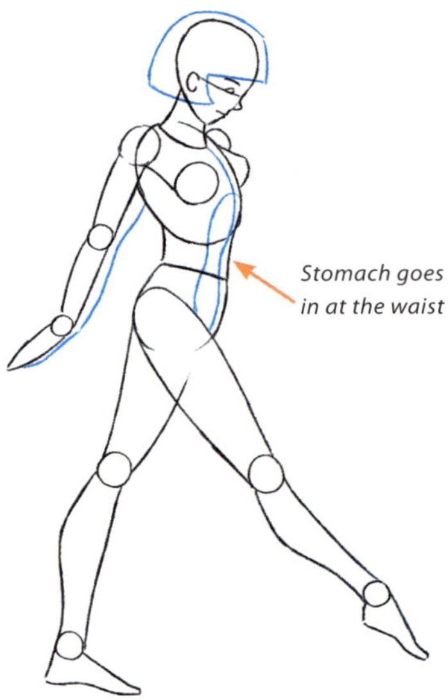

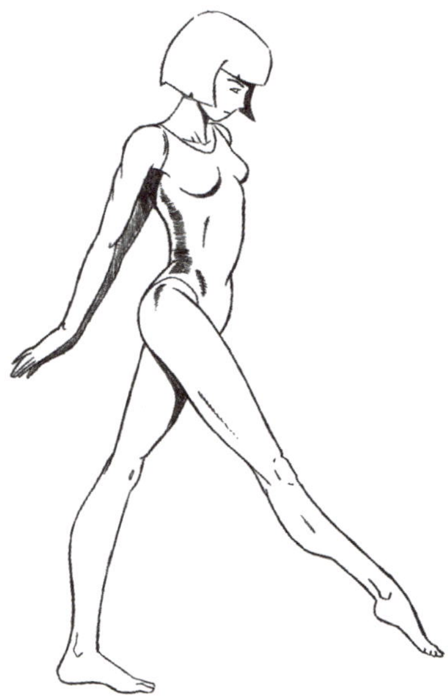

TAKE A HINT!

The muscles and bones of the body form a series of concave and convex curves.

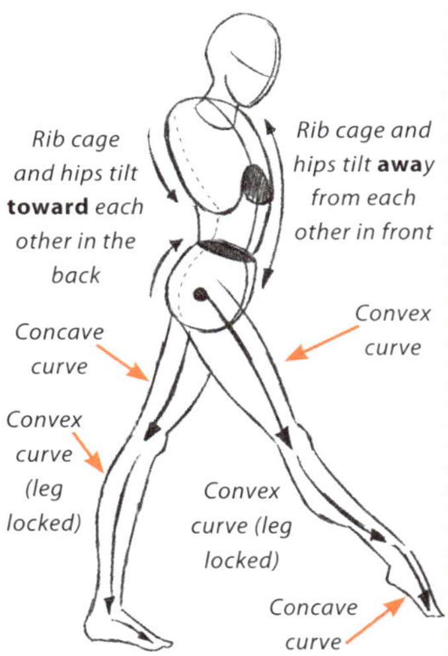

GRACEFUL POSE

Here's a rear ¾-view pose. Because it is a ¾ view, more of one side will face us than the other. The spine, which we all know is in the middle of the body, appears closer to the left than to the right in this pose, due to perspective. We can say that her left side is "diminishing," or, if you prefer, "traveling away from us."

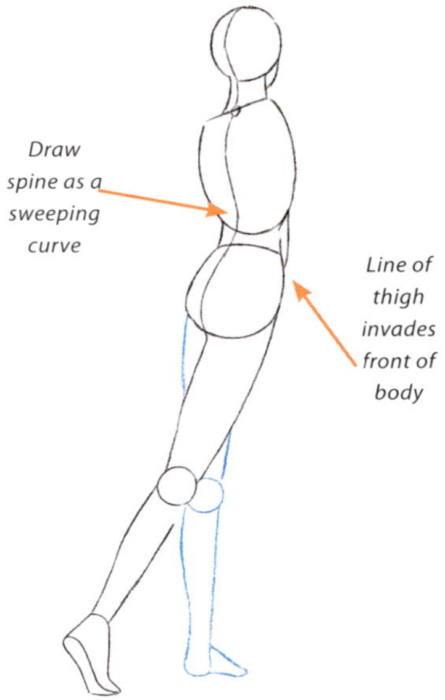

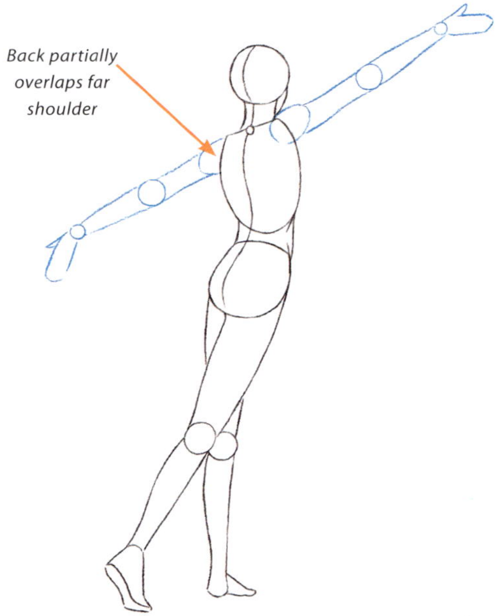

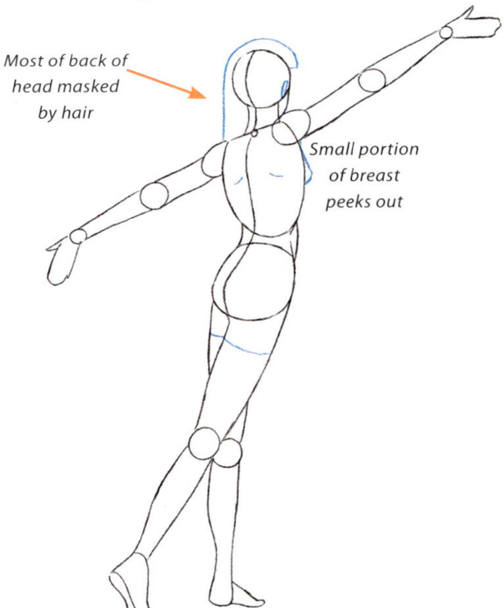

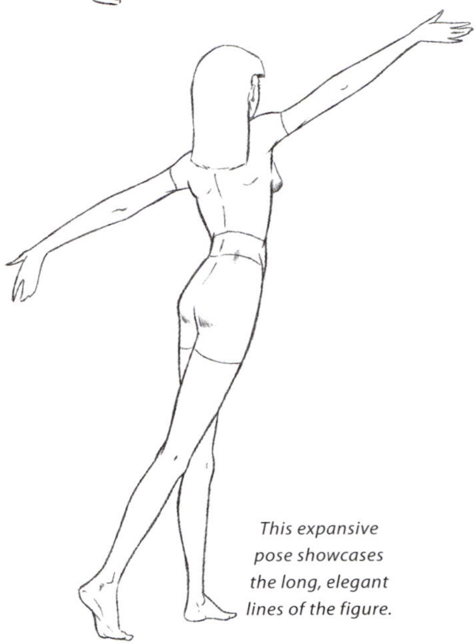

This expansive pose showcases the long, elegant lines of the figure.

YOU TRY IT!

FYI

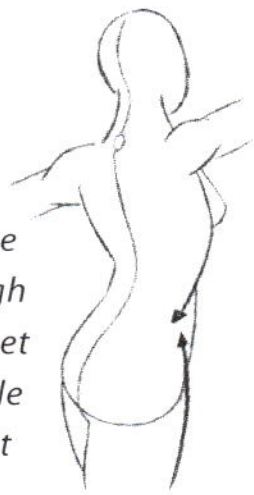

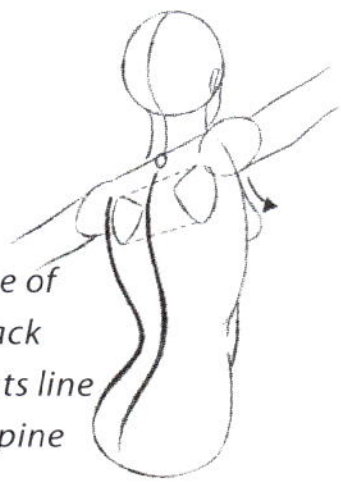

LEANING AGAINST A WALL

Here's a contradictory pose: an elongated, slinky body that is tensed up in order to lean at a 45-degree angle. There are a lot of body dynamics going on here that make for an interesting pose.

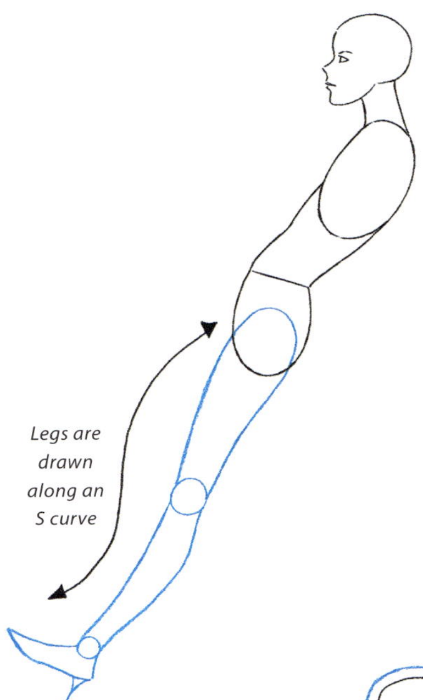

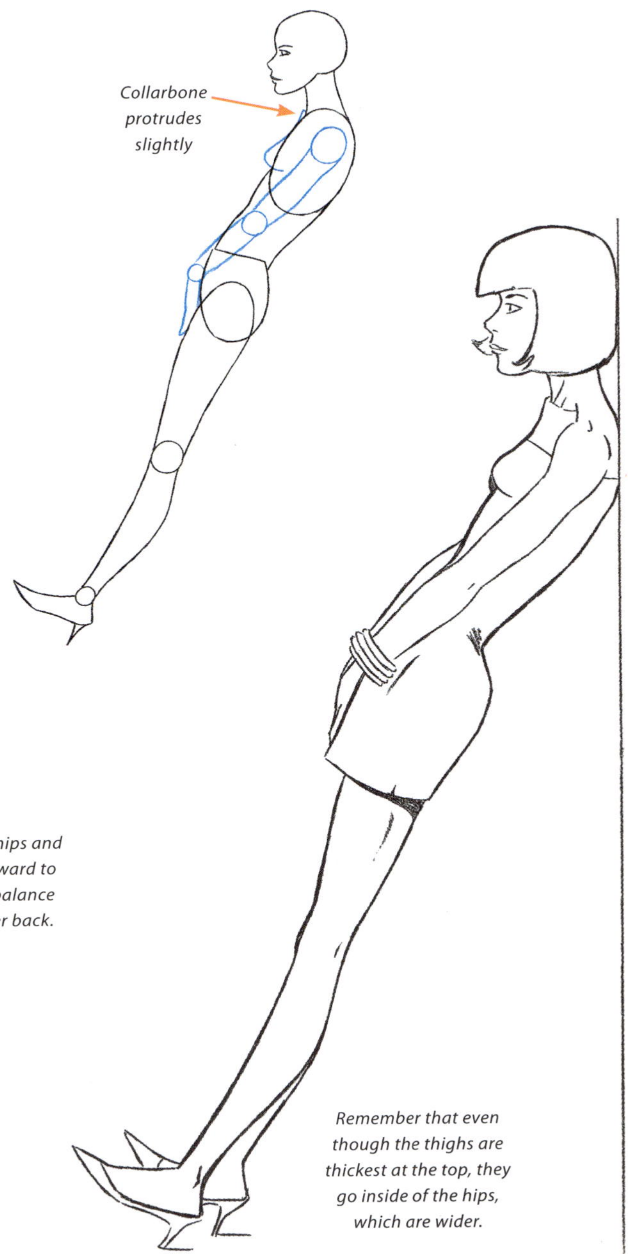

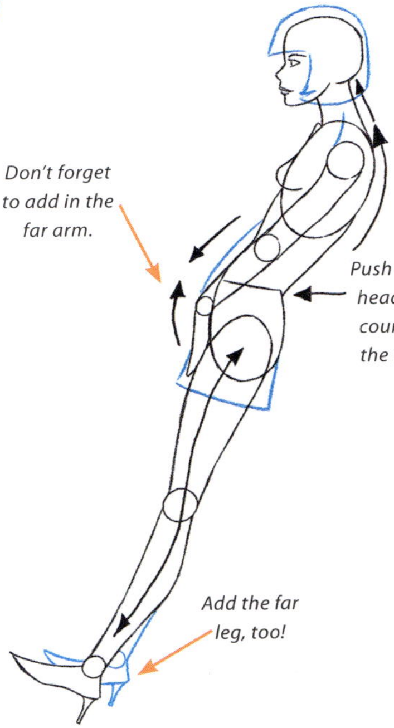

YOU TRY IT!

You may find it helpful to start by drawing a straight, vertical line to represent the wall.

COUNTERPOISE

The arms mirror each other, which is called *counterpoise*. It's a good tool for relating one arm to the other. It's also pleasing to the eye, which intuitively senses the balance.

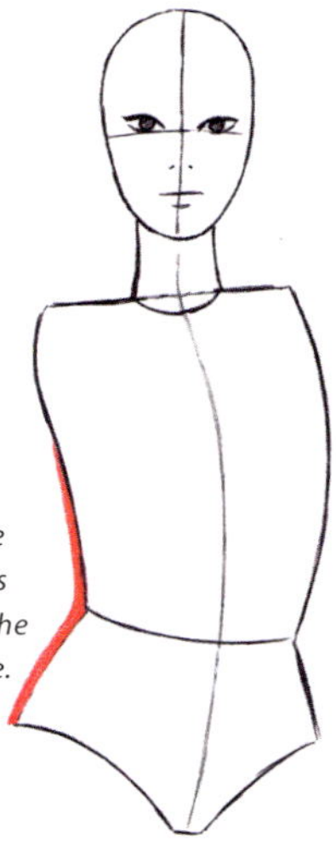

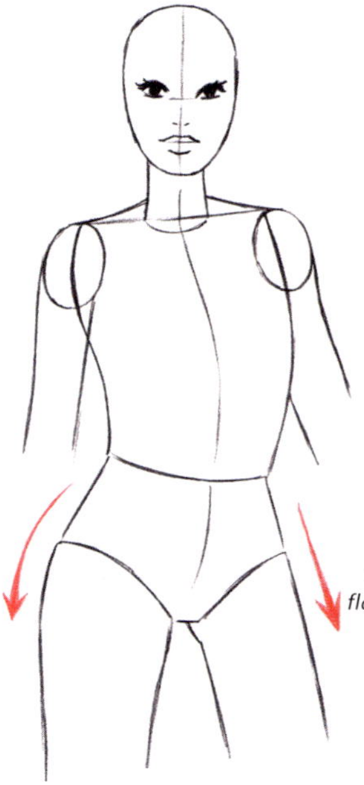

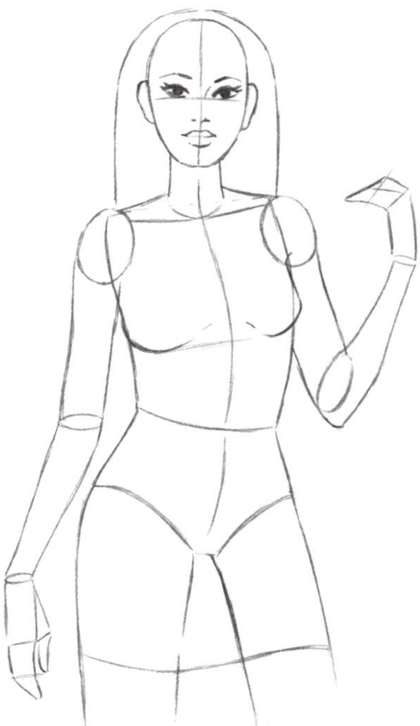

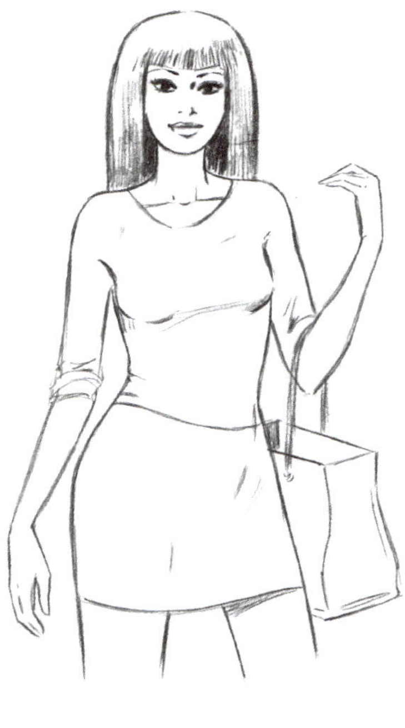

YOU TRY IT!

CROSSED ARMS

Ah yes, I feel your pain. If you've had trouble drawing this arm position, then I've got good news for you. It's actually not a difficult pose—really. But you have to go in order. If you simply draw spontaneously, it can be a beast. Let's try it.

- **A** *Instead of drawing both arms at the same time, completely draw the top arm—the one that will take the dominant position in the final drawing.*
- **B** *Draw the second arm under the first arm.*
- **C** *Draw the entire second arm, even the part that will ultimately be erased (blue lines).*
- **D** *The elbows dip. The arms cross in the center of the torso.*

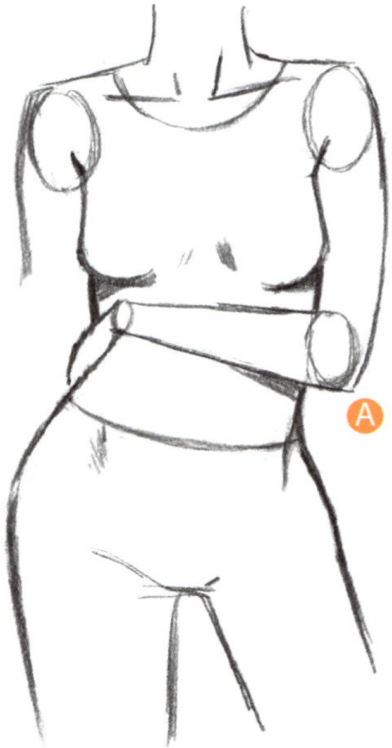

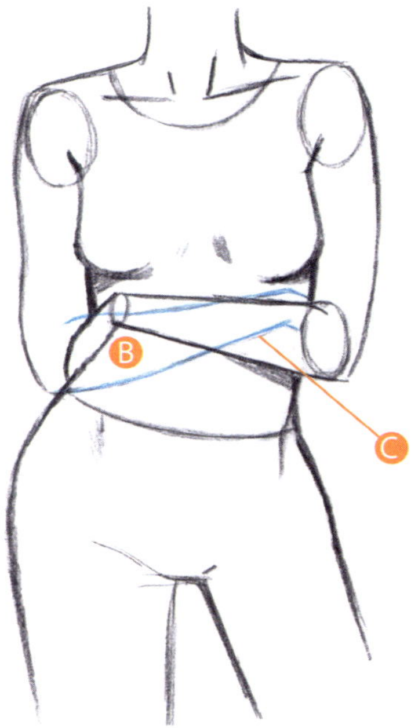

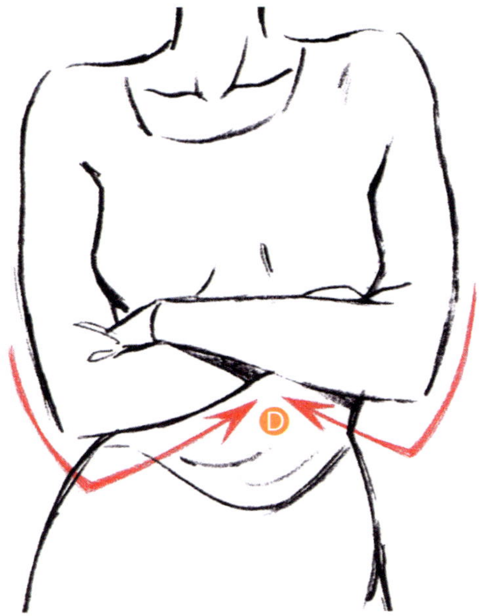

YOU TRY IT!

Practice drawing crossed arms in the space below. We'll look at them as part of a full figure on the following page.

CROSSED ARMS—FULL POSE

Following the simple steps we learned from the previous page, we'll apply the same sequence to drawing crossed arms on a complete figure. And here's the takeaway: Establish the placement of the torso and hips first. They're the constant. The arms are the variables.

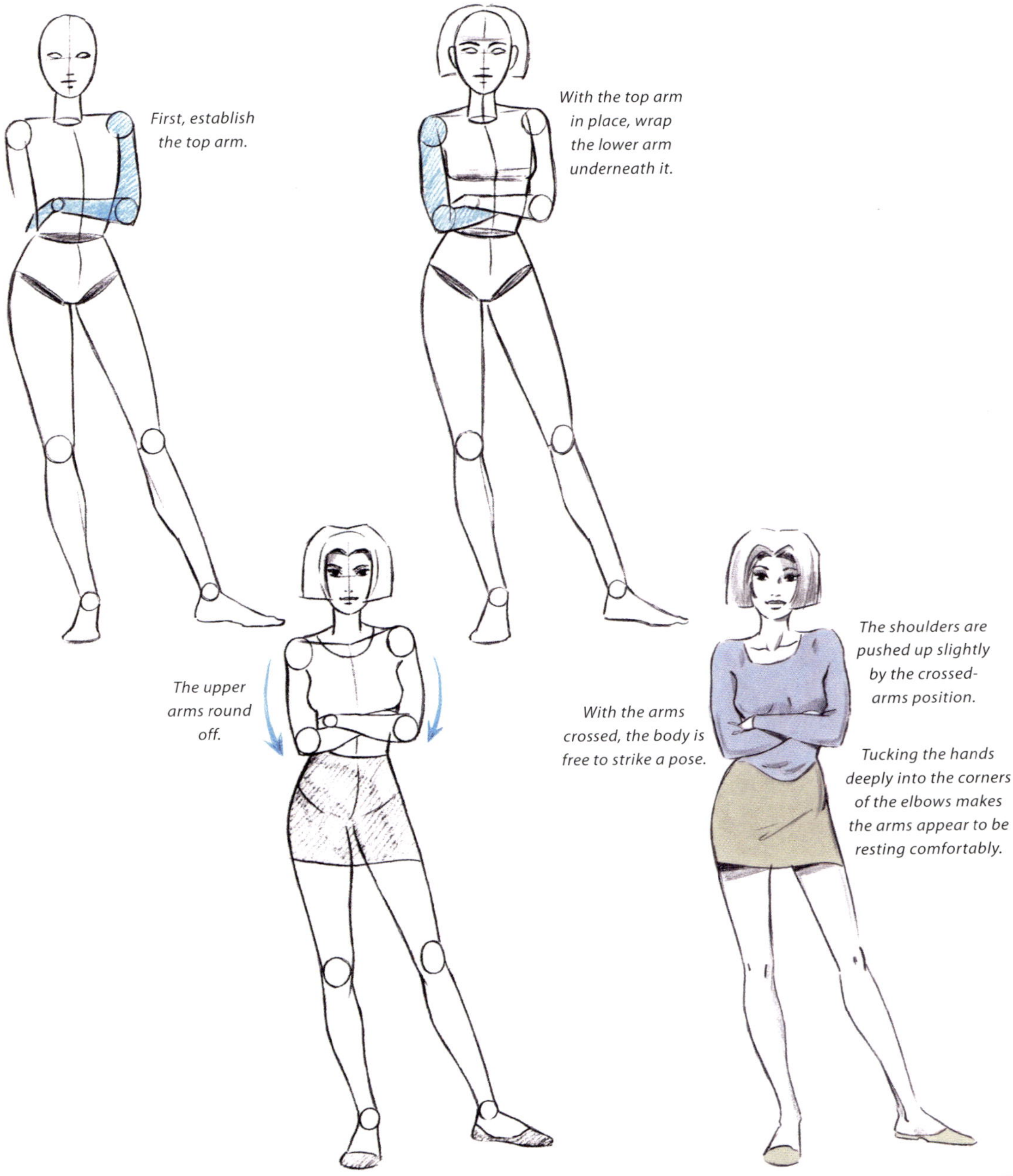

TURNING THE FEET

Here's a technique you can use to add an accent to your drawings. Start with the feet at shoulder-length apart. That's a pretty standard stance, but not one that really stands out. Now, draw the same stance, but turn the feet so that the toes point slightly inward. As a result of this small adjustment, the pose becomes stylish and playful.

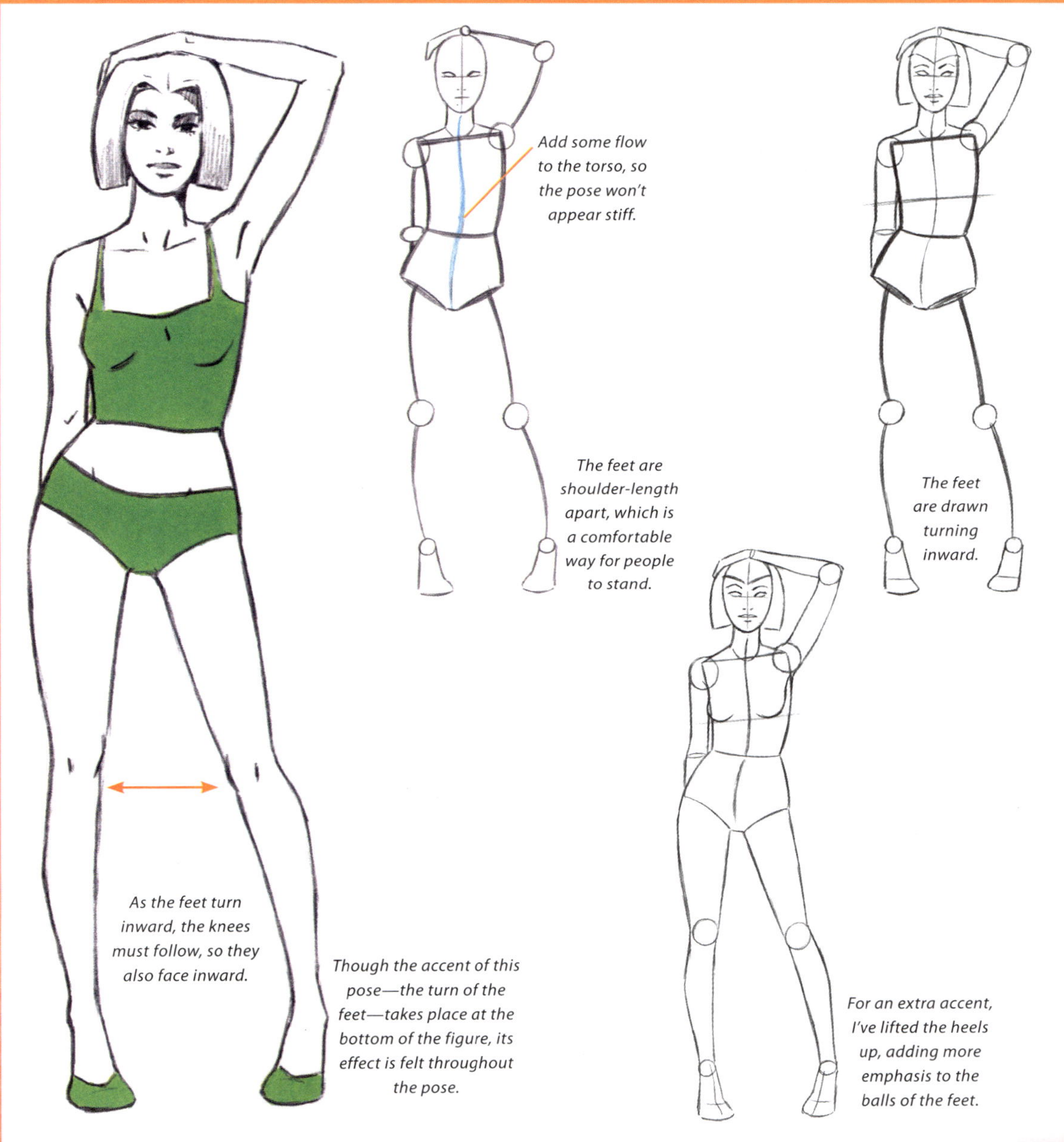

POSE POINT

Turn the feet only enough to begin a slight curve inward.

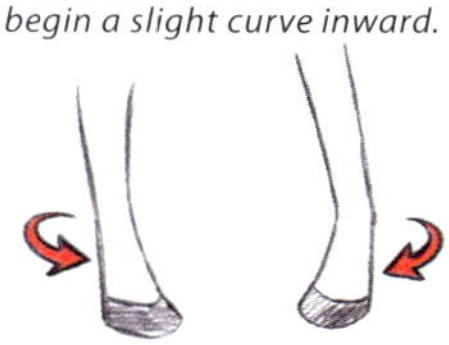

BENDING THE LEG

It can get redundant if you draw the legs side by side. It's often more effective if you were to draw one knee out in front of the other. If both knees were drawn together, the far knee would appear hidden behind the near knee, and the result would be a flat look.

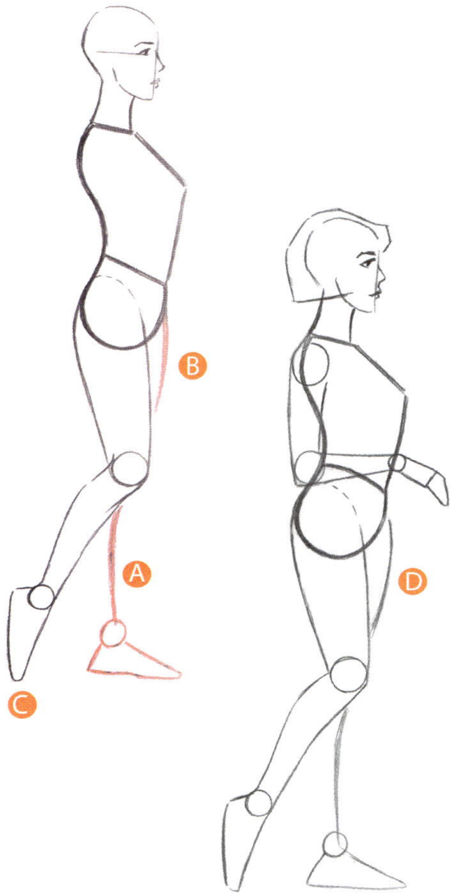

- **A** *Foundation leg*
- **B** *The near knee goes past the far knee.*
- **C** *Figure balances on tip of toe*
- **D** *Far thigh is visible*

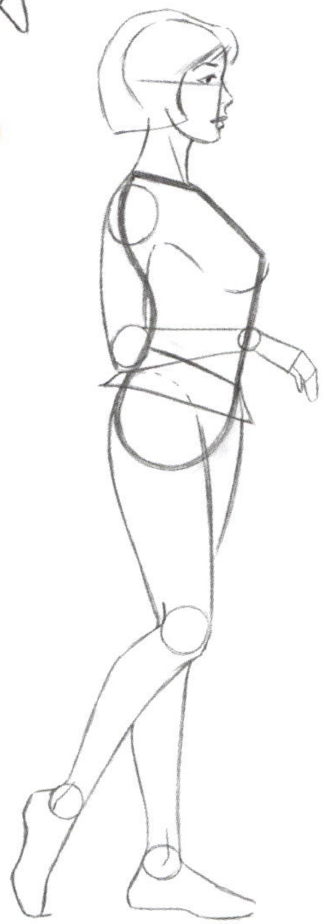

Finished Construction

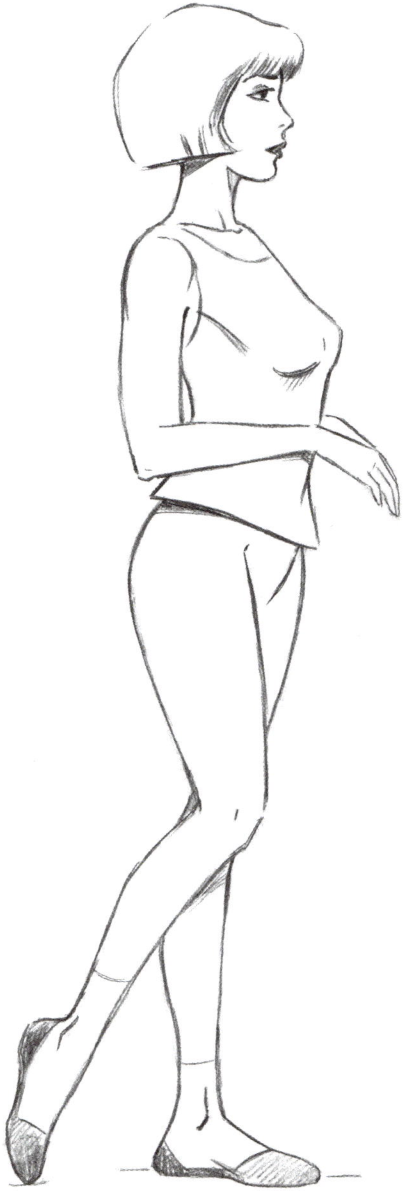

Finished Pencil Sketch

YOU TRY IT!

SITTING ON THE GROUND

When the figure sits on the ground and leans back without an assist from a chair, the arms do the work that the legs do in a standing pose: they prop up the body. Let's look at some of the dynamics that this brings into play.

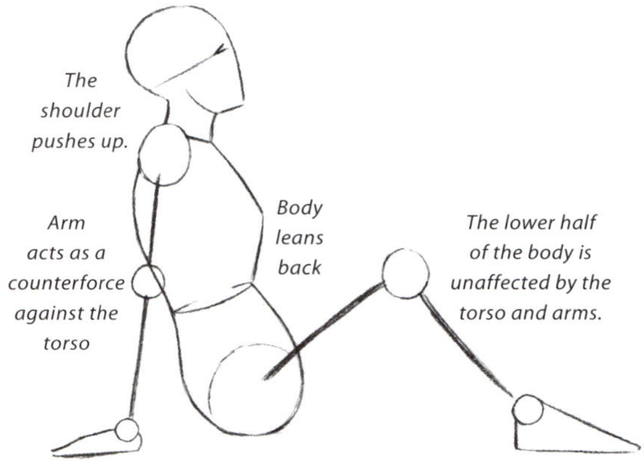

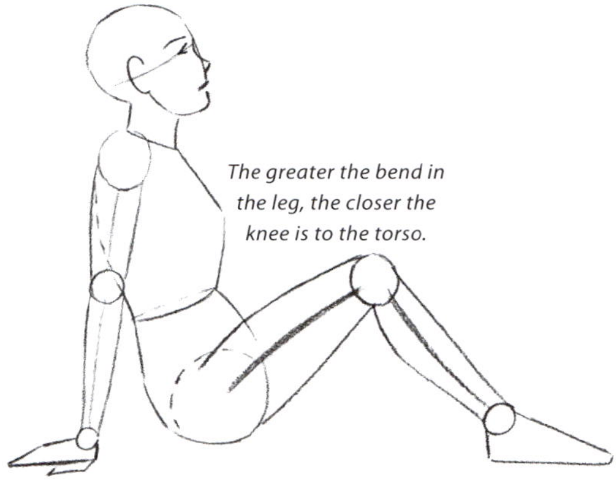

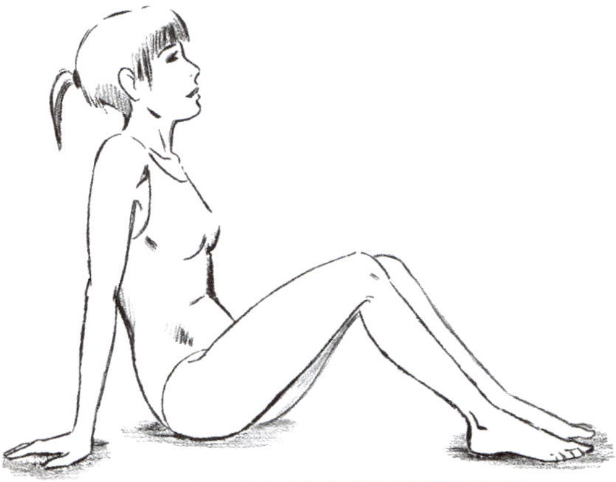

Finished Construction

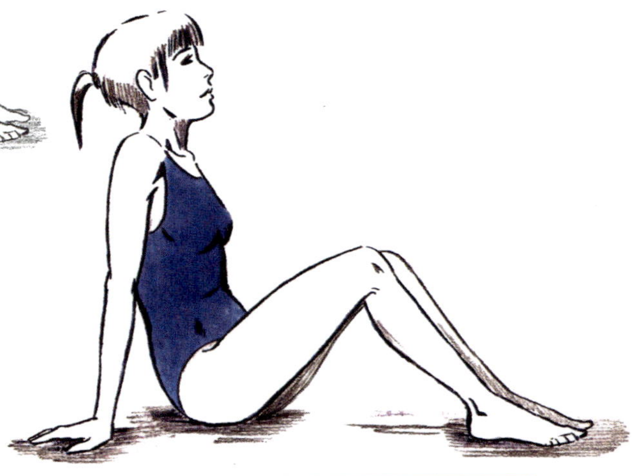

Finished Drawing with Tone

YOU TRY IT!

SITTING WITH LEGS TOGETHER

If this pose has given you trouble before, it soon won't. By focusing on the basic construction, we can see how achievable it is. First, we need to be specific about which parts of the body make contact with the surface of the bench.

Creating the Sitting Area

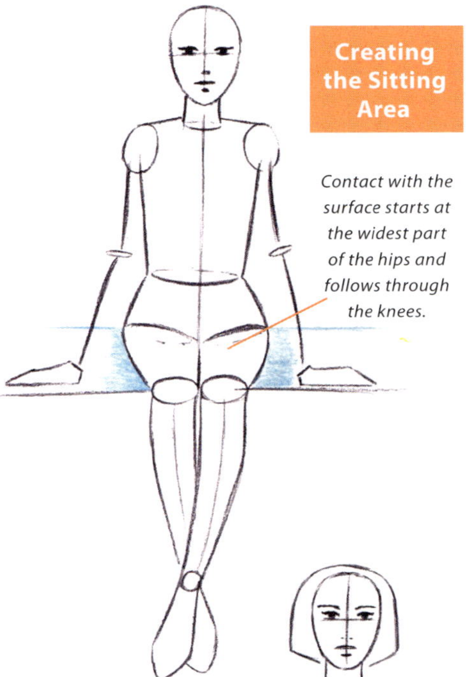

The Three Directions of the Figure

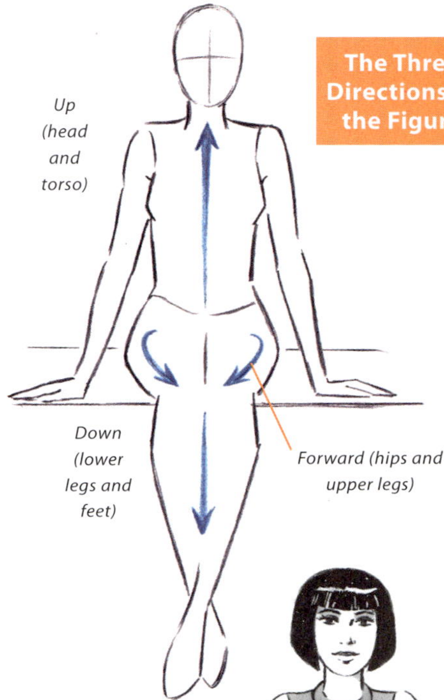

Adding Detail

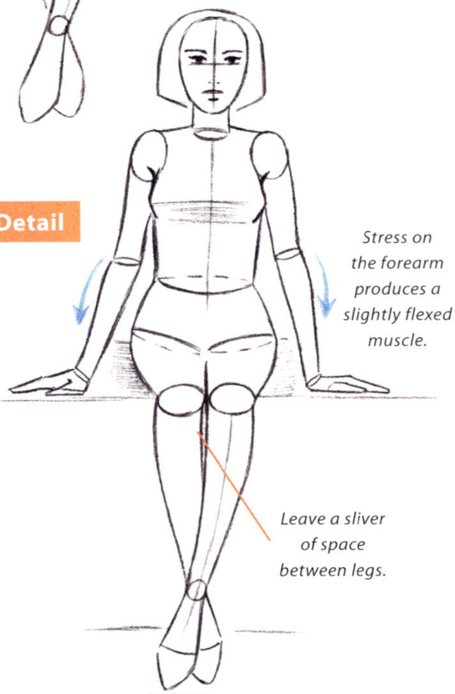

The Viewer's Eye Position

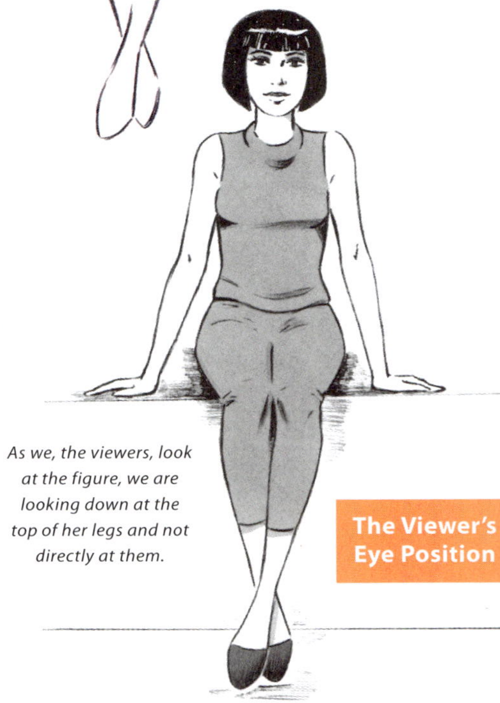

ANGLE OF HIPS

The angle at the base of the hips widens and then angles inward toward the knees.

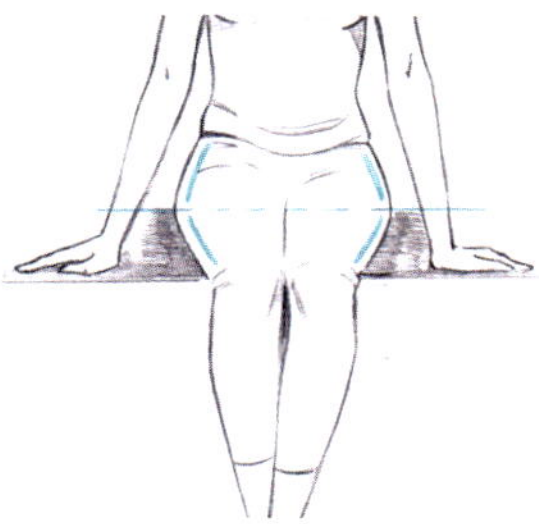

The blue horizontal line represents the back of the bench, and therefore its width.

Blank pages for freehand sketching

DRAWING MEN

Generally, the muscles of the male physique are more developed and articulated than they are on the female figure, though the body mechanics remain the same.

CLASSIC STANDING POSE

One of the main differences between female and male torsos evident in this simple standing pose is the waistline. On males, it's lower and not as pronounced. And notice that the rib cage tends to be larger on men. There's just a look of more width overall.

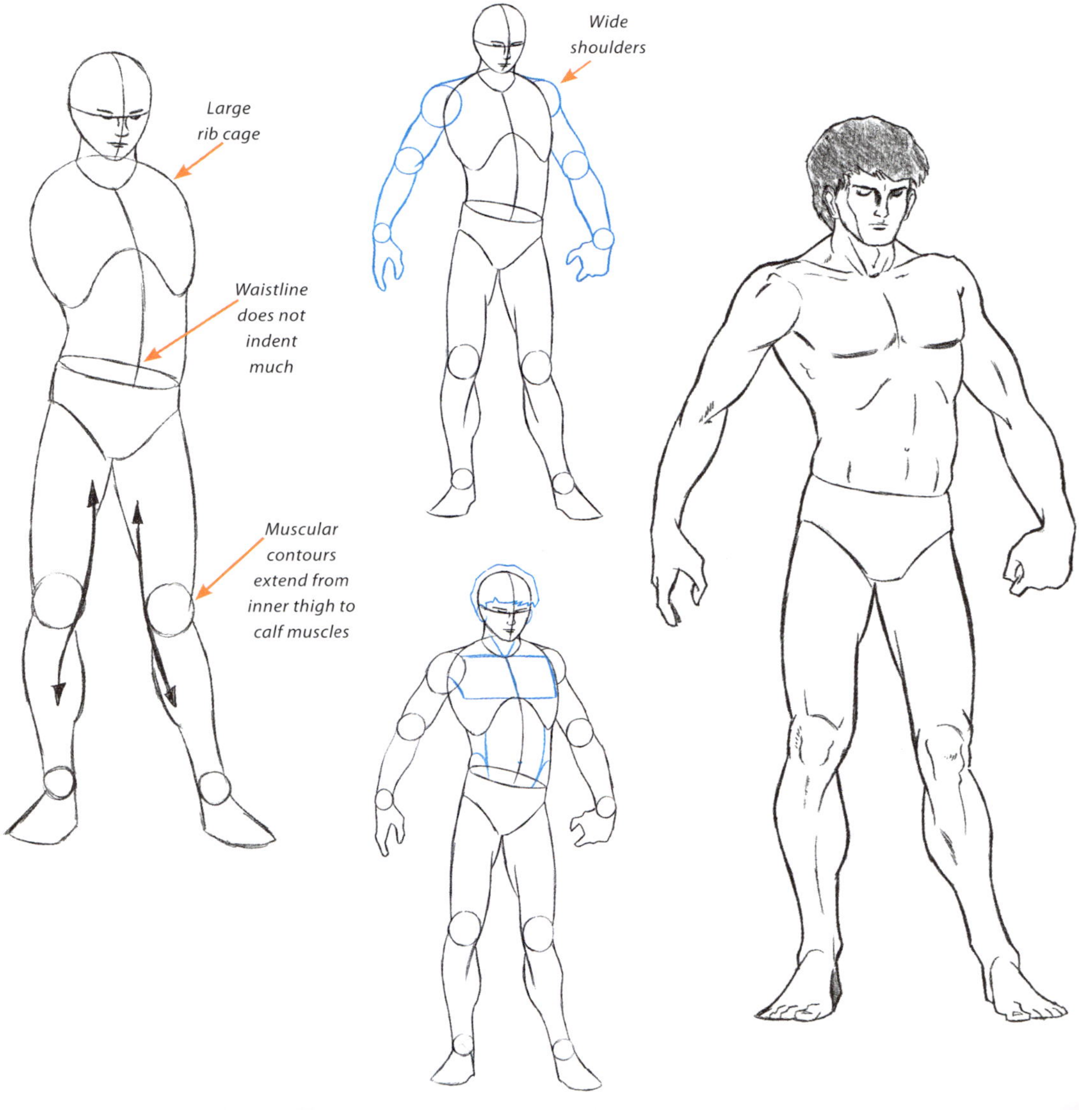

YOU TRY IT!

TAKE A HINT!

When a person is standing facing forward, the natural stance of the feet is a 45-degree angle.

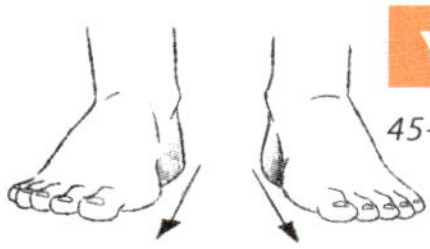

YES!

45-degree angles

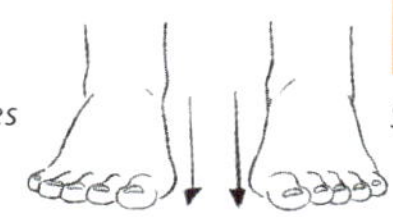

NO!

Straight ahead

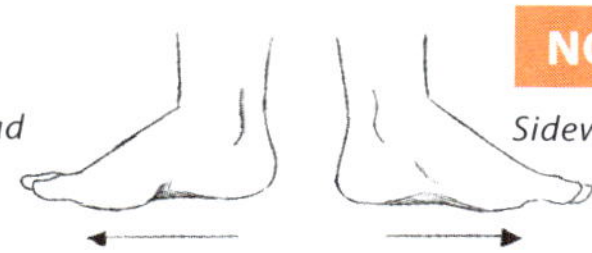

NO!

Sideways

BACK VIEW WITH HANDS ABOVE HEAD

In this pose, the muscles of the upper back contract in a very specific way, creating a simple and predictable muscle pattern. Drawn correctly, the back muscles look convincing and strong.

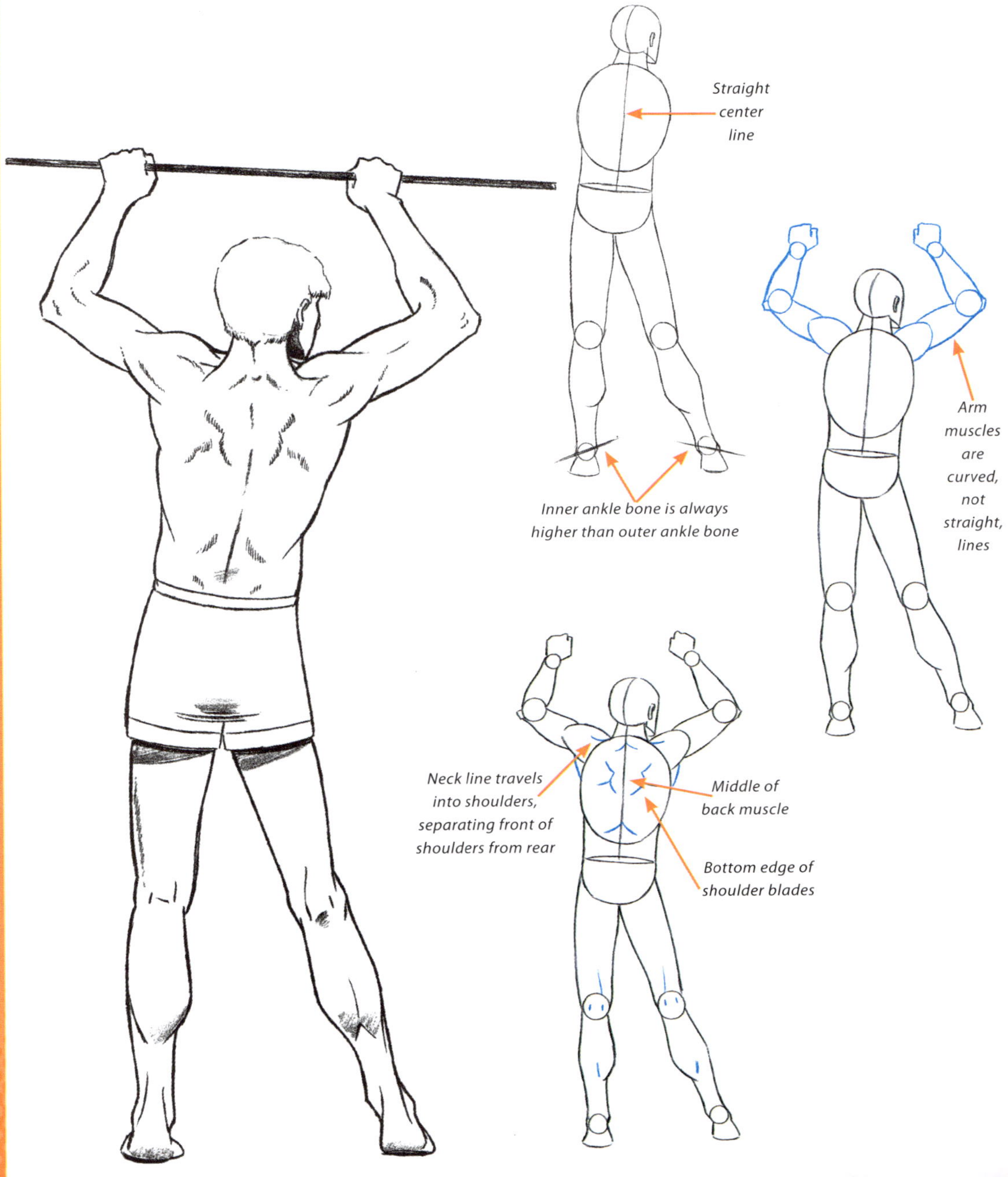

TAKE A HINT!

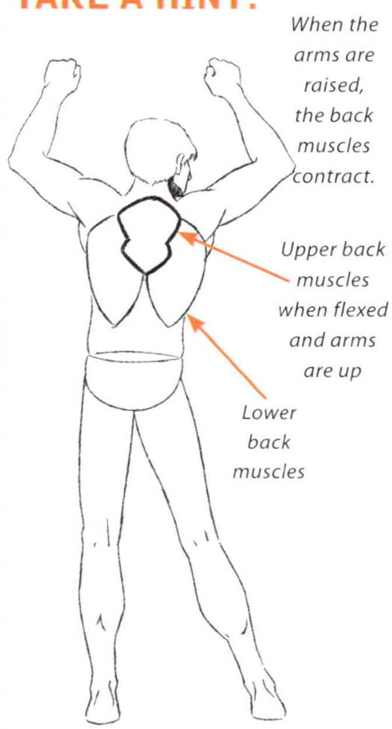
When the arms are raised, the back muscles contract.
Upper back muscles when flexed and arms are up
Lower back muscles

HEROIC POSE

Heroic figures have been drawn, painted, and sculpted throughout history. These days, there's a lot of demand for excellent figure-drawing work in commercial art, and comics now employ fine artists who really know how to portray heroic anatomy. When drawing an athletic character, define the muscles clearly.

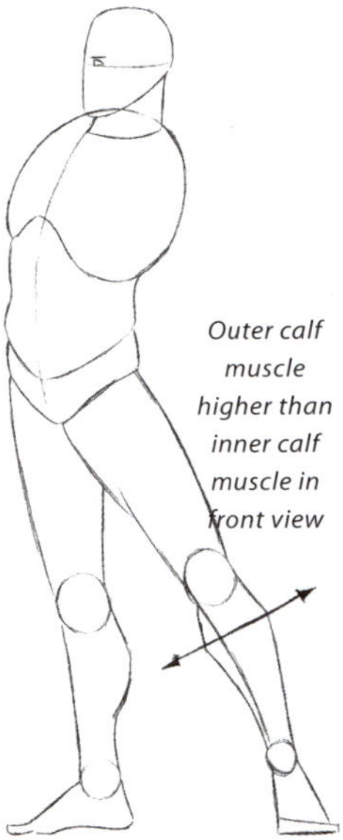

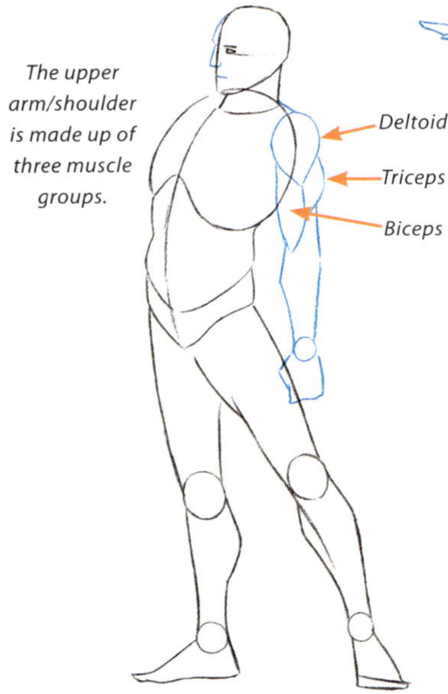

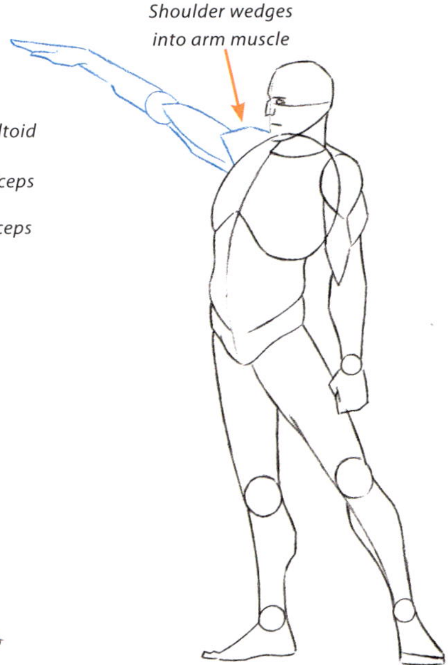

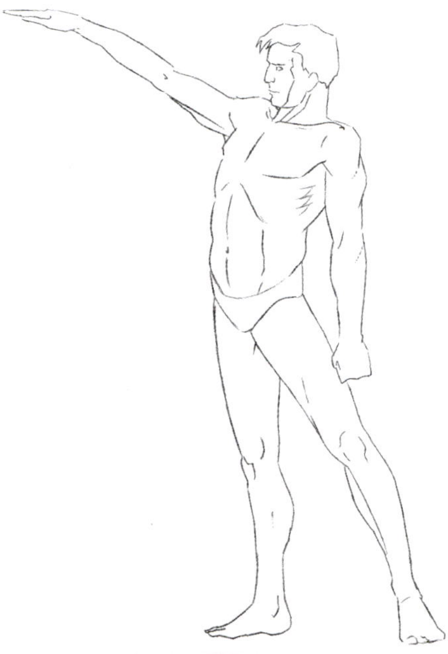

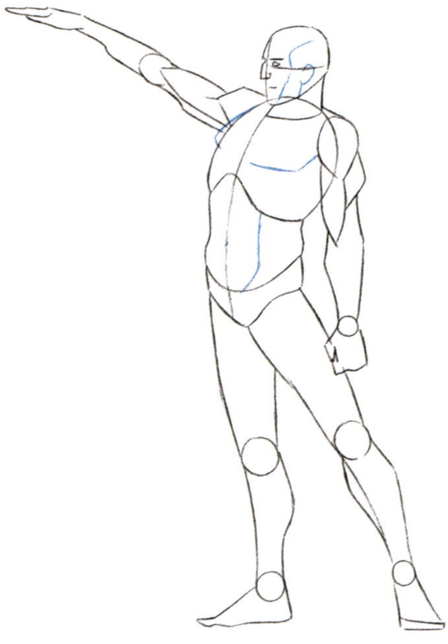

TAKE A HINT!

The movements of the palm and the biceps are linked.

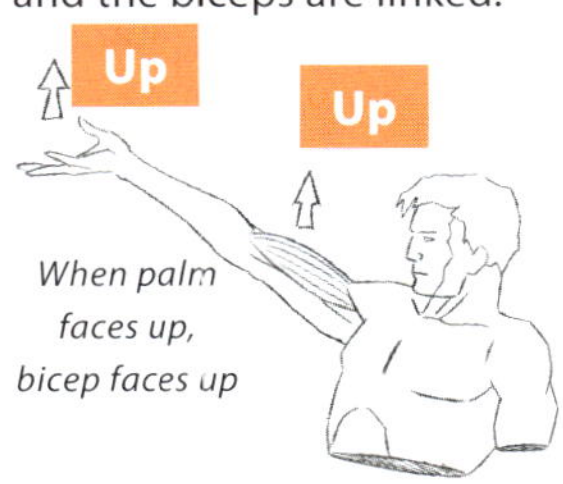

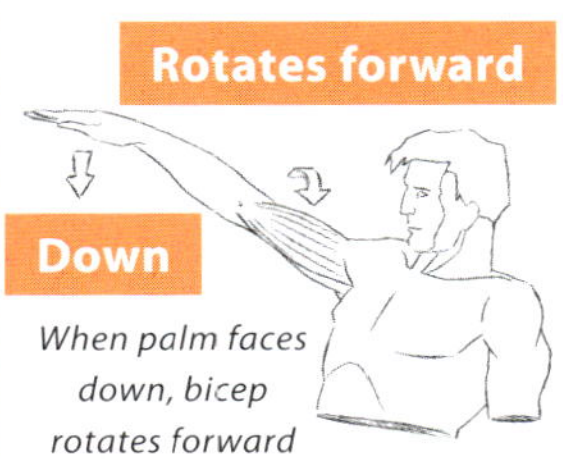

OLYMPIC STANCE

This is the physique of a trained athlete. His trunk twists as if he's pulling a bow and arrow, resulting in some interesting dynamics that make the pose come alive. The trunk is in a ¾ front pose, yet we are viewing the back of the head, and the legs are in a side view! This seamless combination of angles adds a nice sense of flow to the figure.

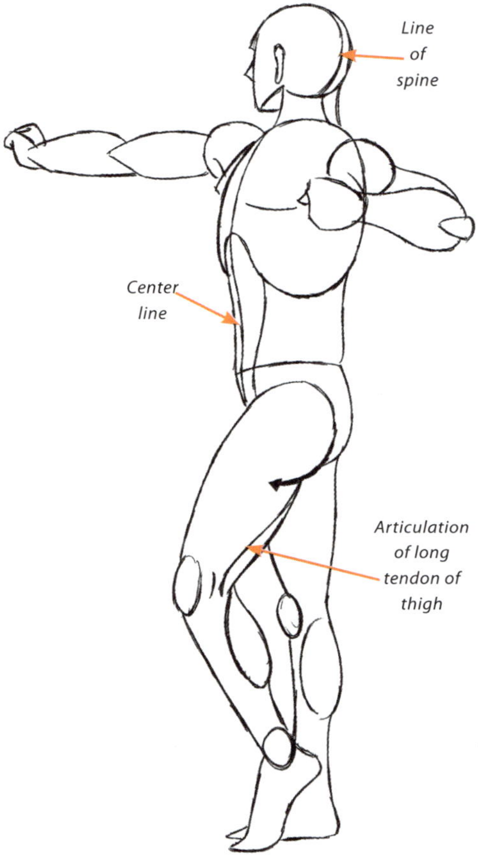

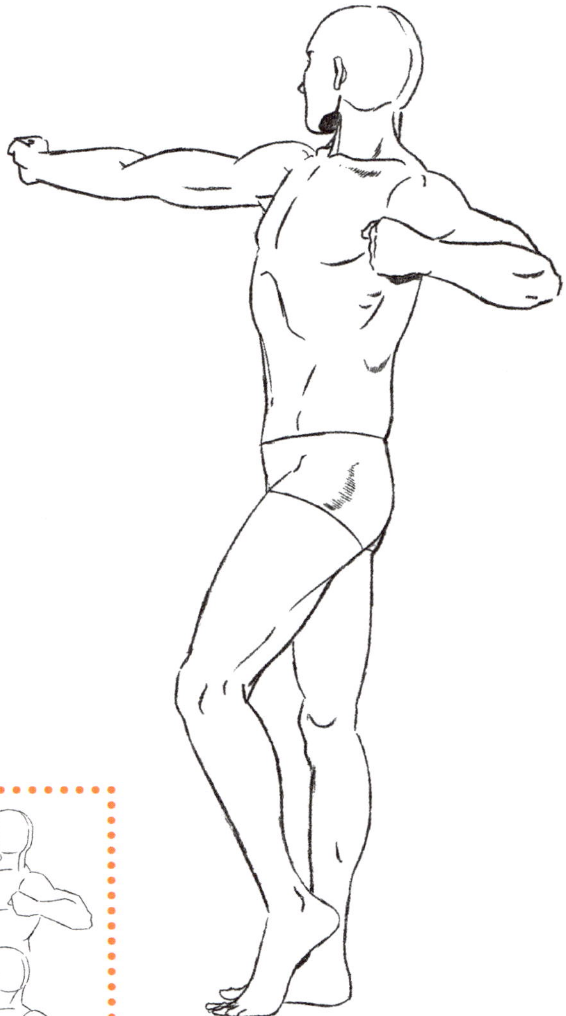

TAKE A HINT!

The arm is traveling away from us and is shortened due to perspective.

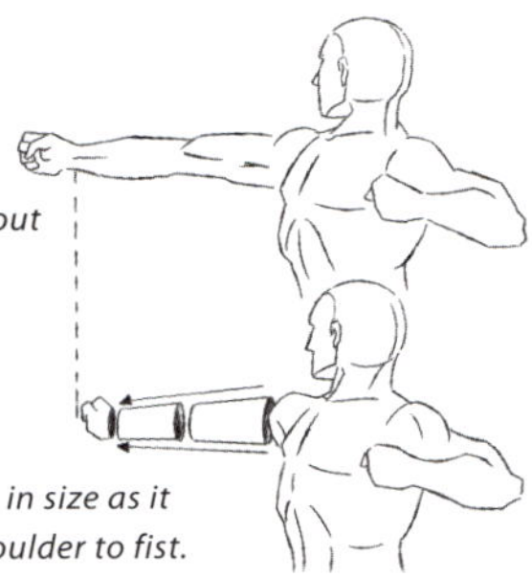

YOU TRY IT!

BEND AND STRETCH

When an athlete bends, his muscles are even more apparent. Aim to blend one muscle group into another so that they flow pleasingly. In this pose, the stress point—where the most bending takes place—is just above the waistline, because that's the spot where there is no bone.

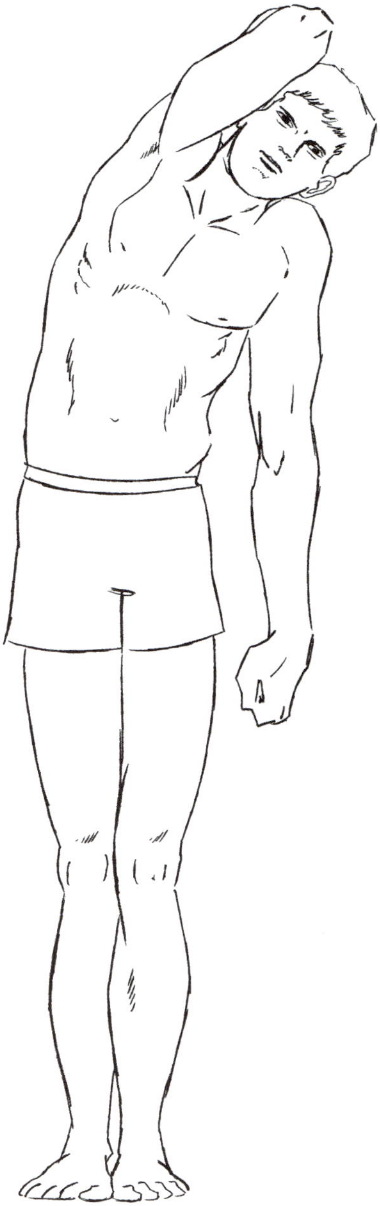

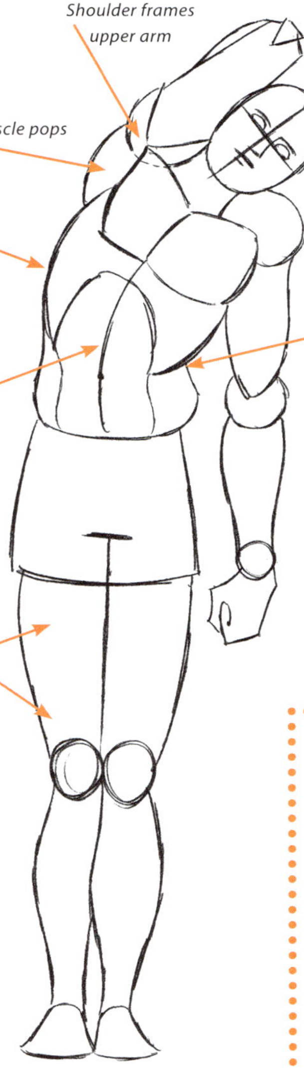

TAKE A HINT!

Note how the back of the arm (triceps) is framed by the shoulder muscles as it tapers down to nothing.

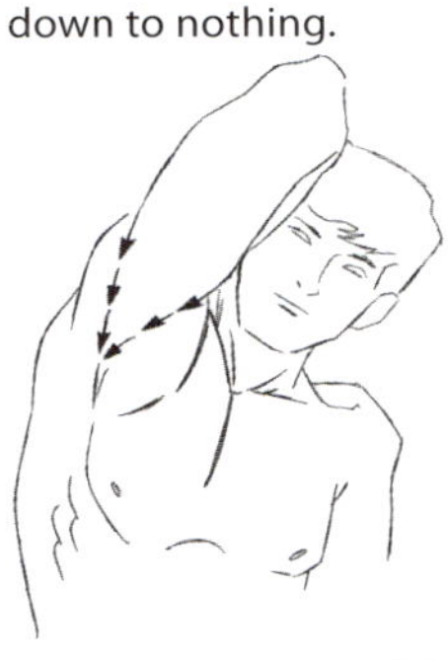

THOUGHTFUL POSE

This is a more wistful pose, as the figure gazes down reflectively. There is also more tilt to the shoulders. This pose's construction is straightforward. The folds and creases in the clothing are not drawn until the last step. To fit the mood of the pose, the figure has a slightly willowy build.

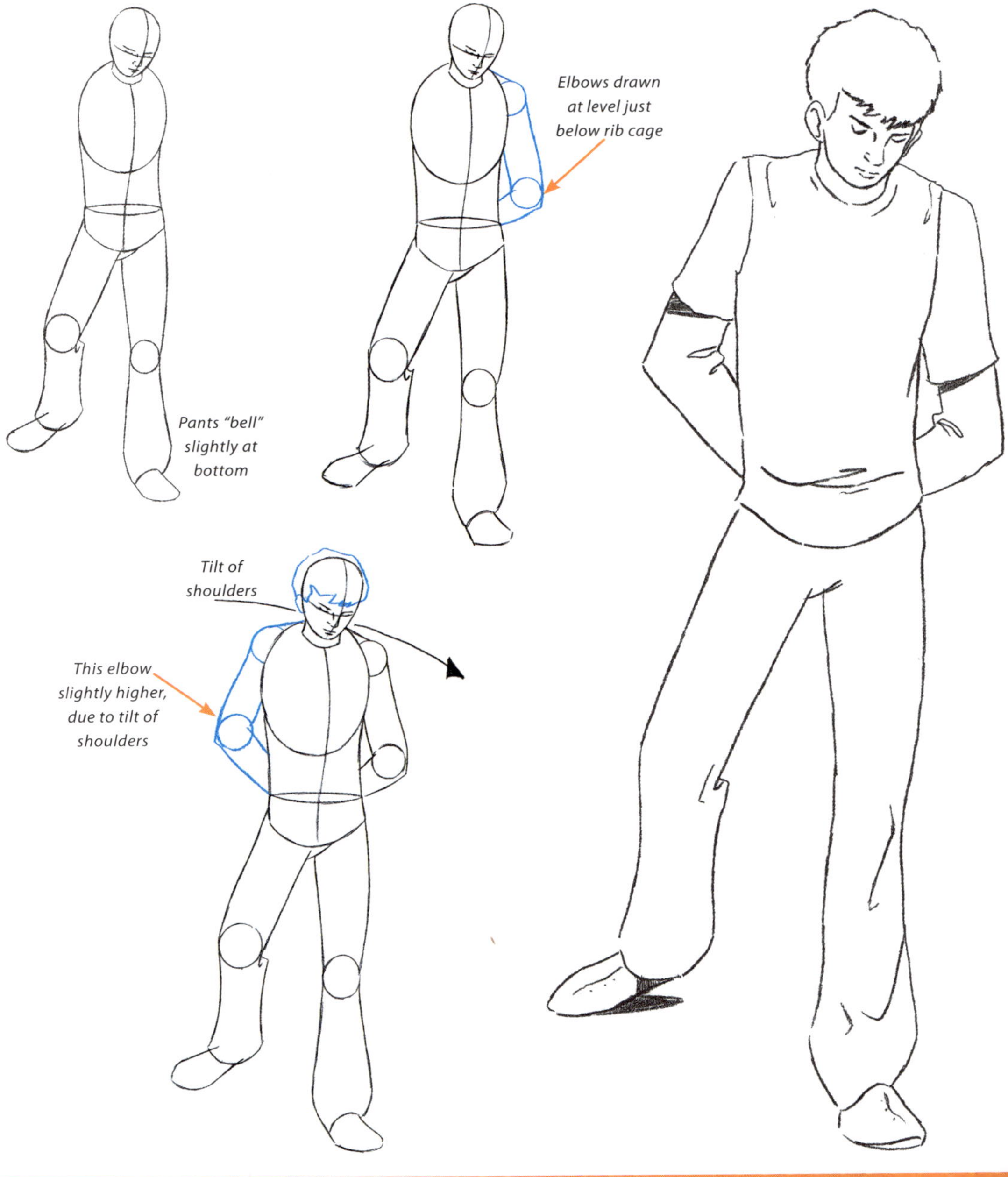

YOU TRY IT!

TAKE A HINT!

The eyebrows curve down when the head faces front and up when the head looks down.

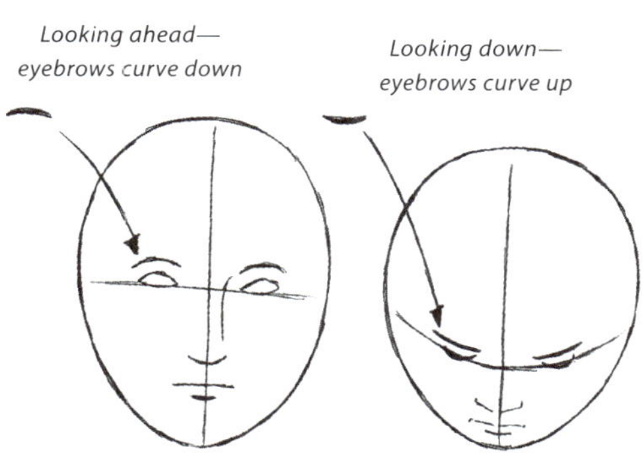

HANDS IN POCKETS—SIDE VIEW

The key to drawing poses is to blend the various sections that make up the body into a pleasing whole. Streamline your poses so that they don't appear to be a series of stacked segments.

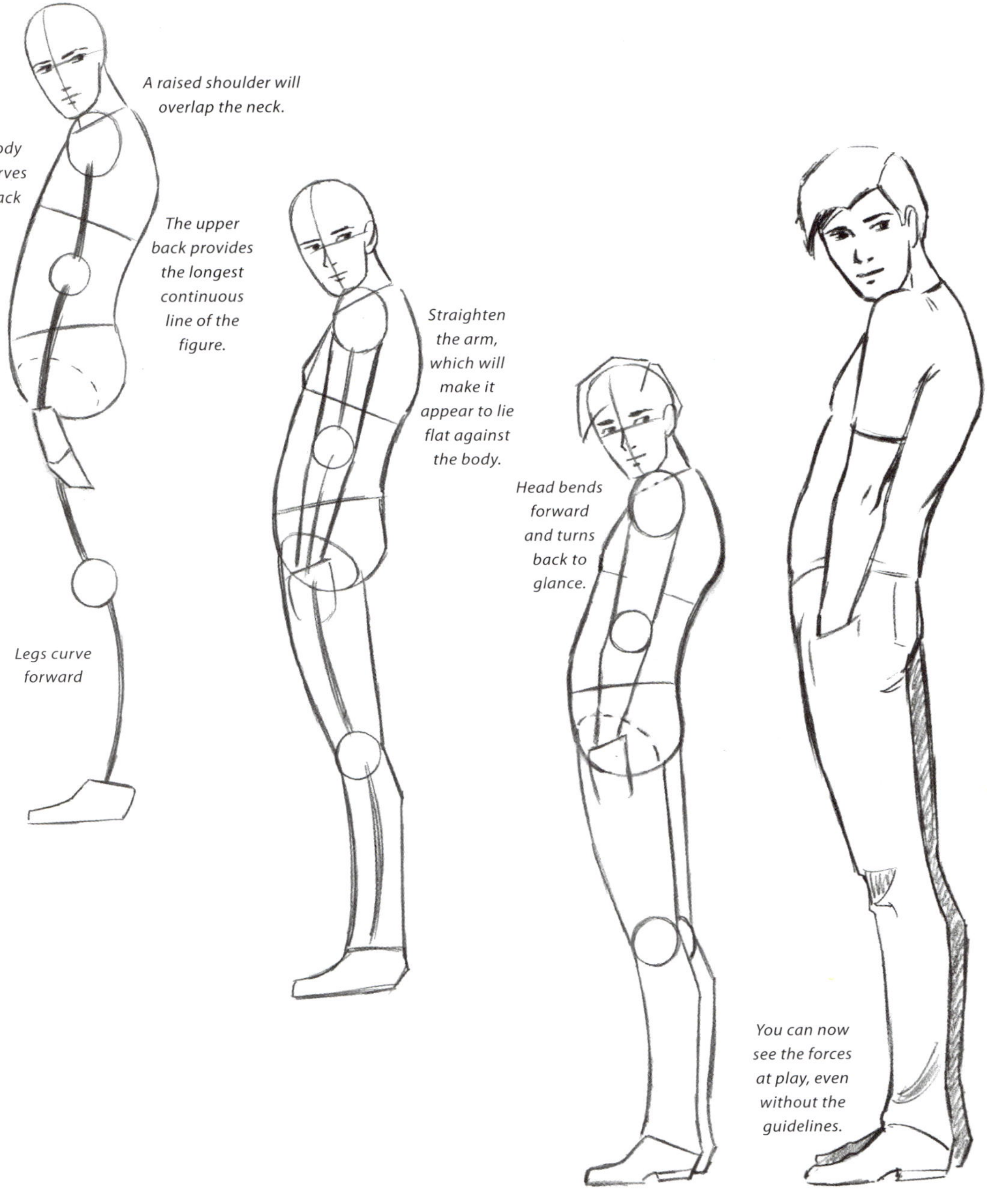

SEATED POSE IN PERSPECTIVE

Look at how compressed that near leg is. That's because it is facing us directly, so it has to flatten out completely due to foreshortening. It sounds impossible, I know, but it's all about the technique. Many of us assume that foreshortening something correctly is a complicated and intricate process. No, it is a process of simplification. And counterintuitive as it may seem, it's actually easy.

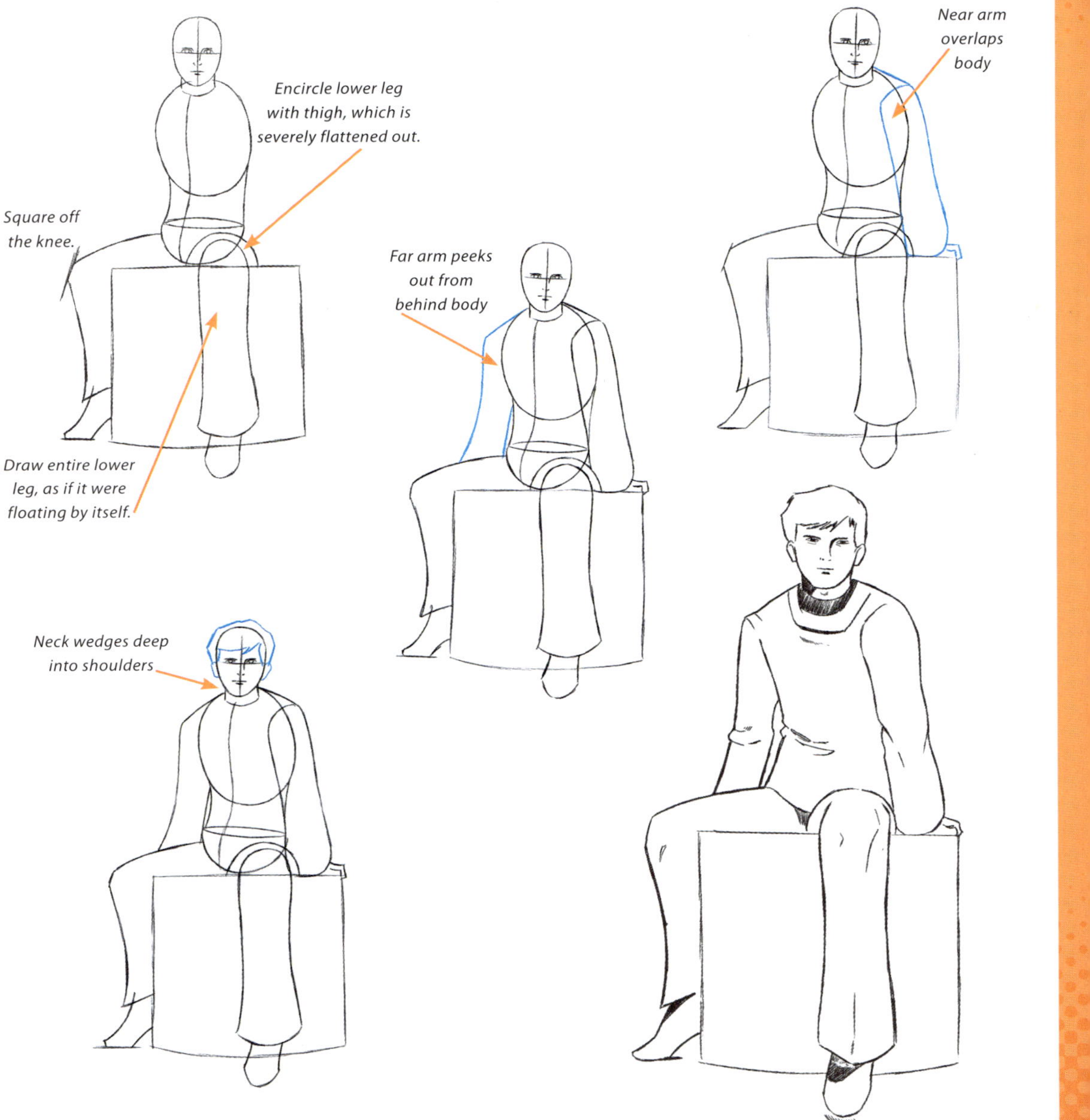

YOU TRY IT!

SITTING IN A CHAIR—SIDE VIEW

If we turn the chair just a few inches to the left, we suddenly have depth. We can keep the same basic position of the torso as in a strict side view while creating variety with the arm and legs.

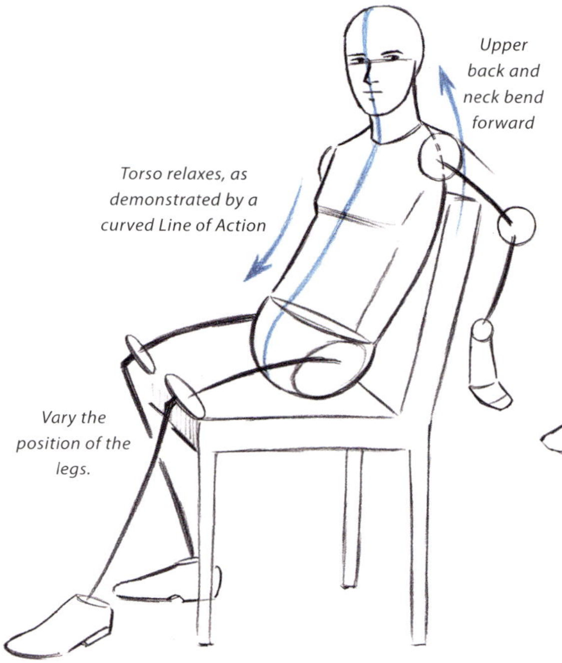

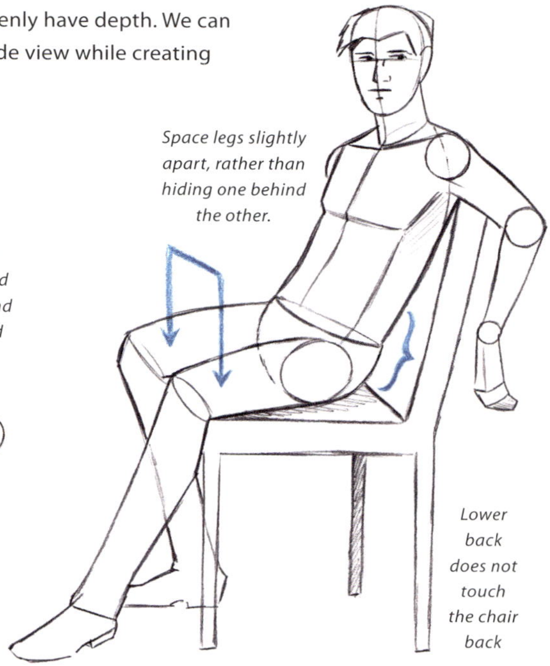

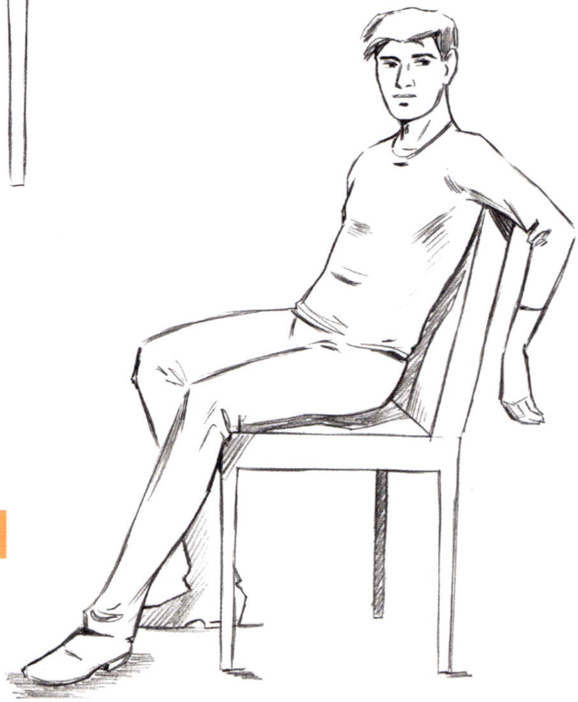

SITTING IN SIDE VIEW

The side view of a figure seated in a chair gives you the clearest view of the position of the hips and legs on the chair.

YOU TRY IT!

TURN A POSE INTO AN ACTION

In this final male pose, we'll turn a basic pose into a common action.

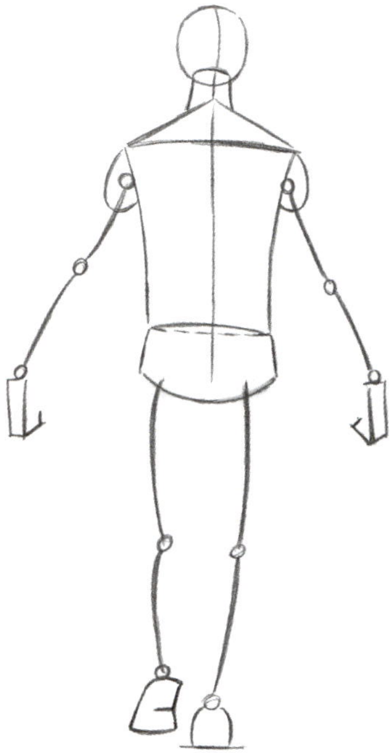

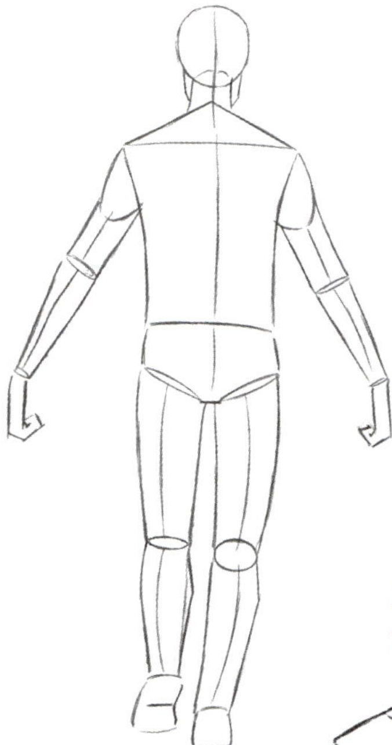

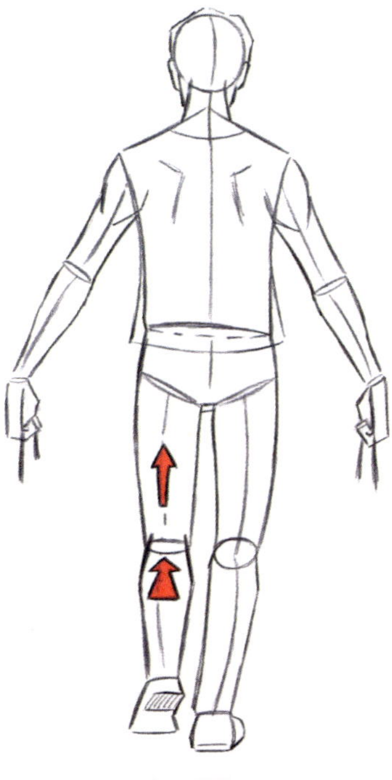

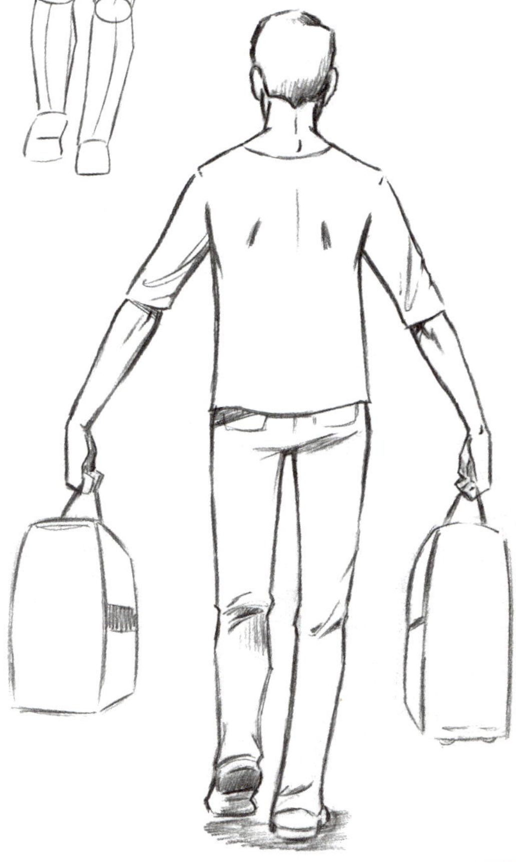

Blank pages for freehand sketching

DEPTH

In this final section, you'll learn to fine-tune your figure drawings by adding depth to create the look of three dimensions. Some poses are naturally flat looking, but we don't have to be constrained to that. There's a lot we can do to create a round look, so that our figures appear more convincing.

DEPTH IN THE SIDE VIEW

This angle creates the flattest view of the figure, but there are various ways to enhance it. The first way makes no adjustment to the line drawing whatsoever, but simply applies shadow strategically.

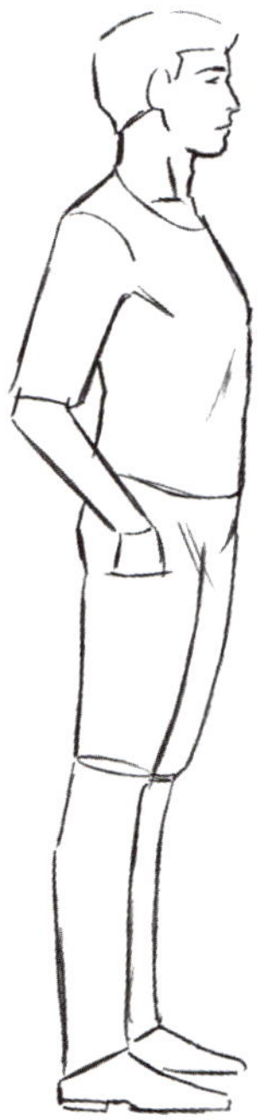

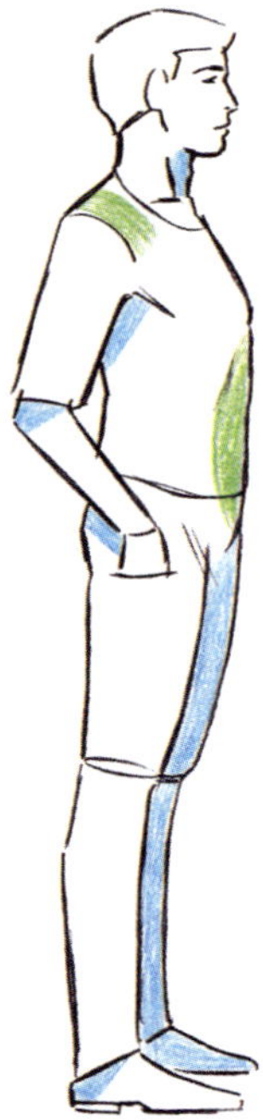

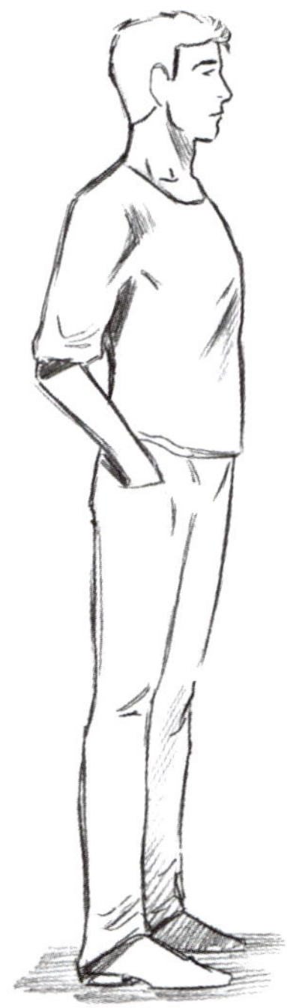

FLAT

This is a line drawing without any consideration to depth. It's a nicely drawn figure, but it has an oddly empty look.

APPLYING SHADOW

The shadow areas are indicated in blue. Notice in each, something blocks the light, casting a shadow. The green areas hint at a different angle, and therefore depth. For example, the figure is in a side view, yet we can see a touch of his stomach and the top of the shoulders. Tone can also be added here.

FIGURE WITH SHADOW

Avoid a heavy-handed approach. A few suggestions of shadow, strategically applied, round out the look.

YOU TRY IT!

First, practice applying shadows to the flat figure below to give it more depth. Then try to draw the figure, with depth, from scratch.

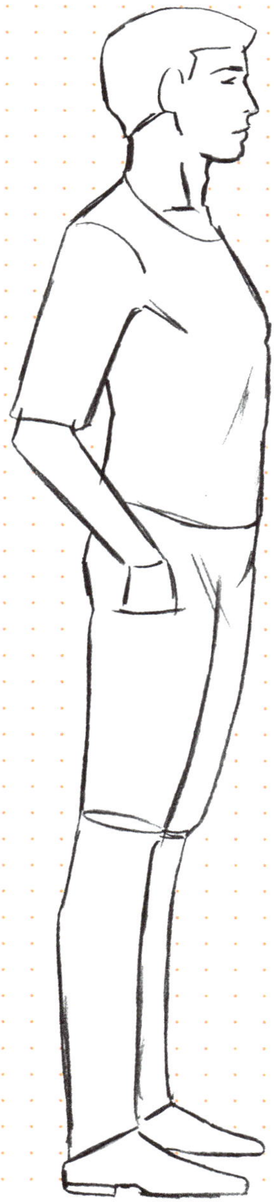

SHIFTING THE CENTER LINE IN SIDE VIEW

In a typical side view, the Center Line (the red guideline) is drawn along the edge of the body, creating the flat look we've just seen. To add depth, move away from a strict side view by shifting the Center Line slightly back from the edge. This has the effect of showing a sliver of the far side of the figure, which suggests depth. In addition, a turn of the head, from a side view to a three-quarter view, also shows depth.

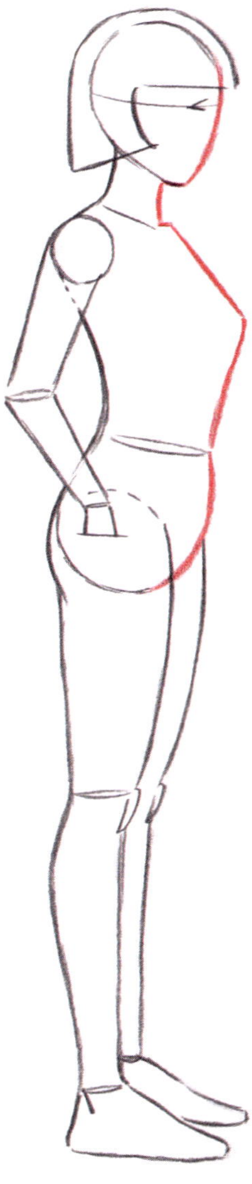

MOVE THOSE FEET!

Beginners have the tendency to draw both feet straight ahead in a side view. But that's not how most people stand. They spread their feet slightly outward. This, too, helps to create a look of depth in the side view.

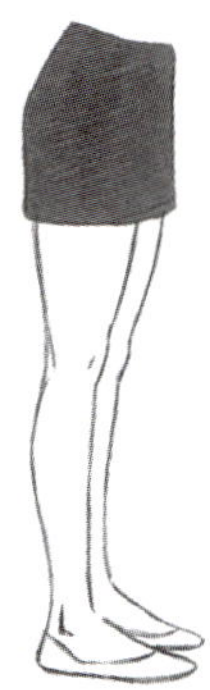

Drawing the feet straight ahead works, but it is a flat look.

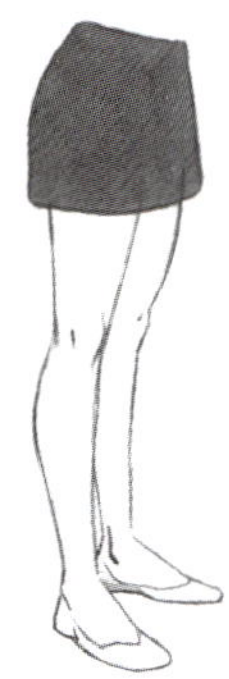

Having the feet angled apart in the side view looks natural and adds depth.

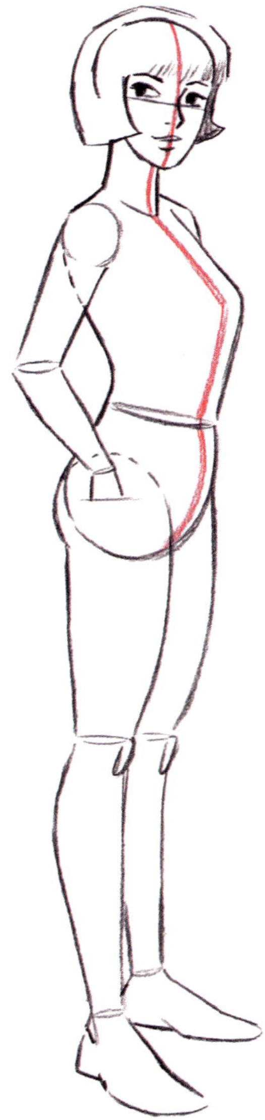

STRICT SIDE VIEW

SIDE VIEW WITH DEPTH

YOU TRY IT!

Adjust the figure below so that the Center Line is shifted to create depth.
Then try to draw the figure yourself from scratch.

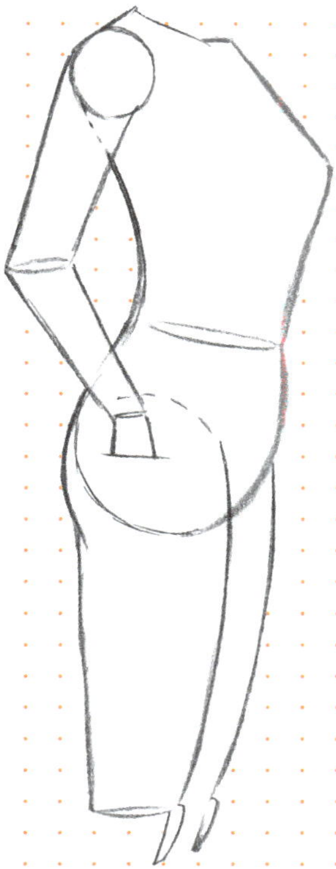

FROM CONSTRUCTION TO FINISHED FIGURE

Now that we've got the concept, let's put the principles into action. We'll build the modified side view, starting from the beginning.

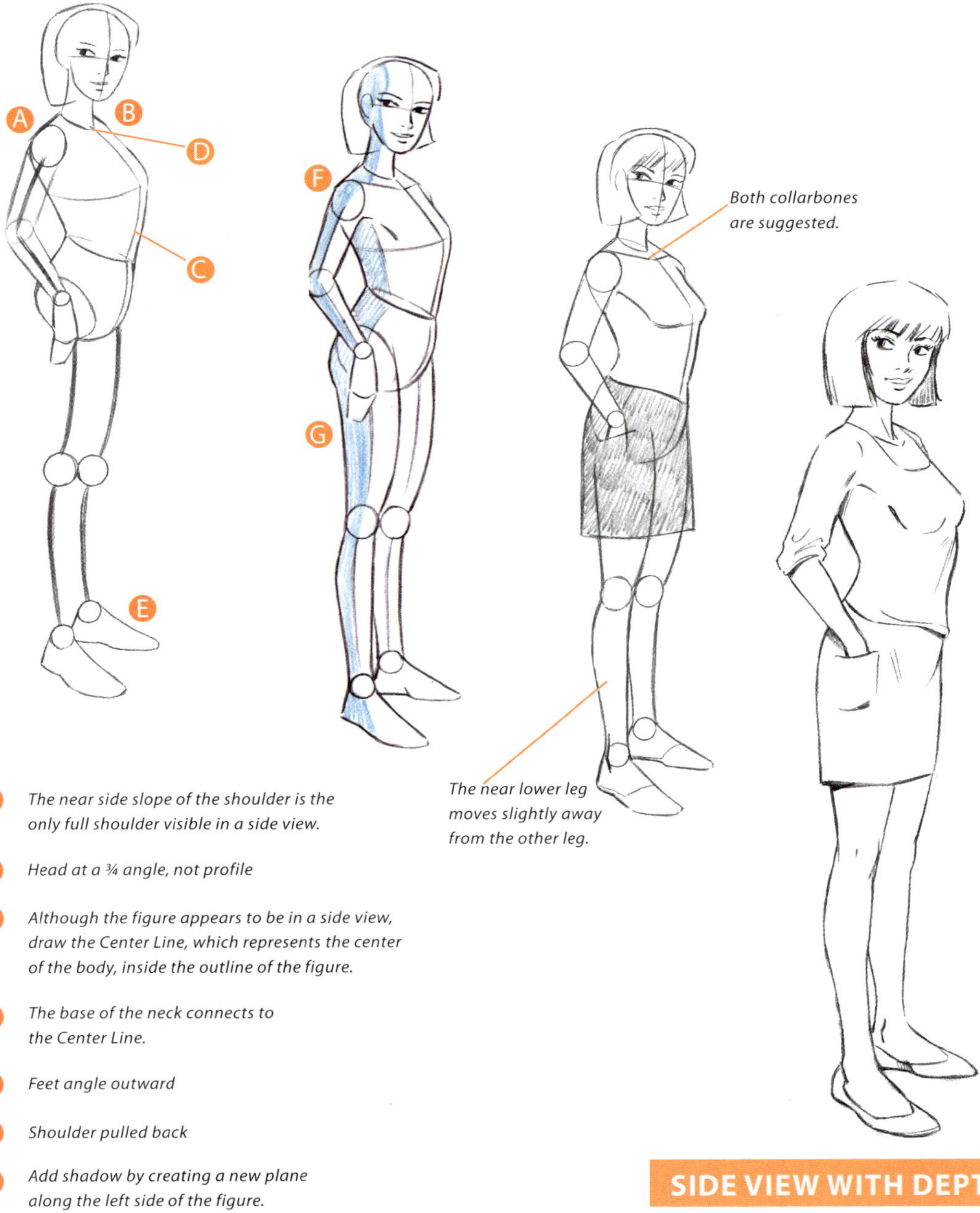

A *The near side slope of the shoulder is the only full shoulder visible in a side view.*

B *Head at a ¾ angle, not profile*

C *Although the figure appears to be in a side view, draw the Center Line, which represents the center of the body, inside the outline of the figure.*

D *The base of the neck connects to the Center Line.*

E *Feet angle outward*

F *Shoulder pulled back*

G *Add shadow by creating a new plane along the left side of the figure.*

OVERLAP AND DEPTH

The phenomenon of overlap is the way our eye instantly recognizes what is nearer to us and what is farther from us. If a car drives in front of a house, we instantly recognize that the car is closer to us than the house. Depth is sensed as the distance between foreground and background objects. The same holds true for figures, but at a much smaller distance, such as when an arm is in front of a torso.

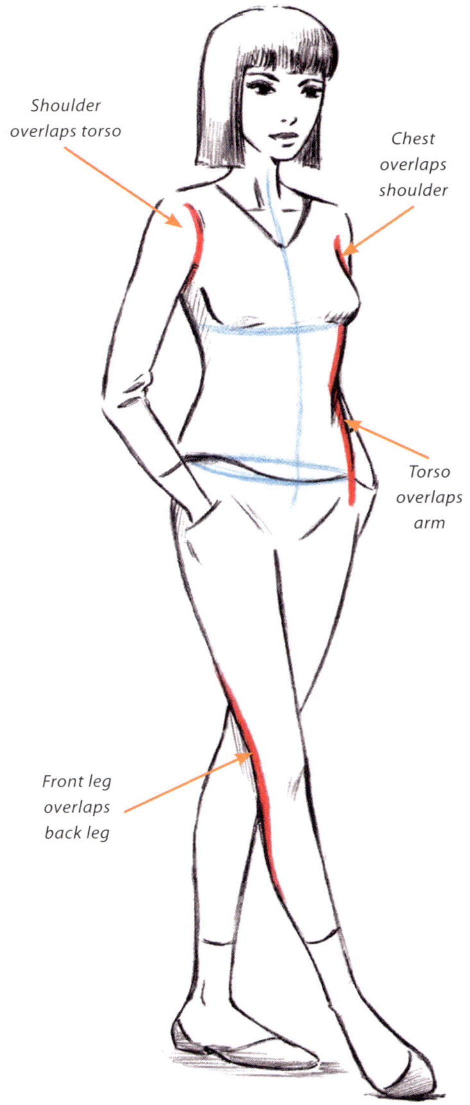

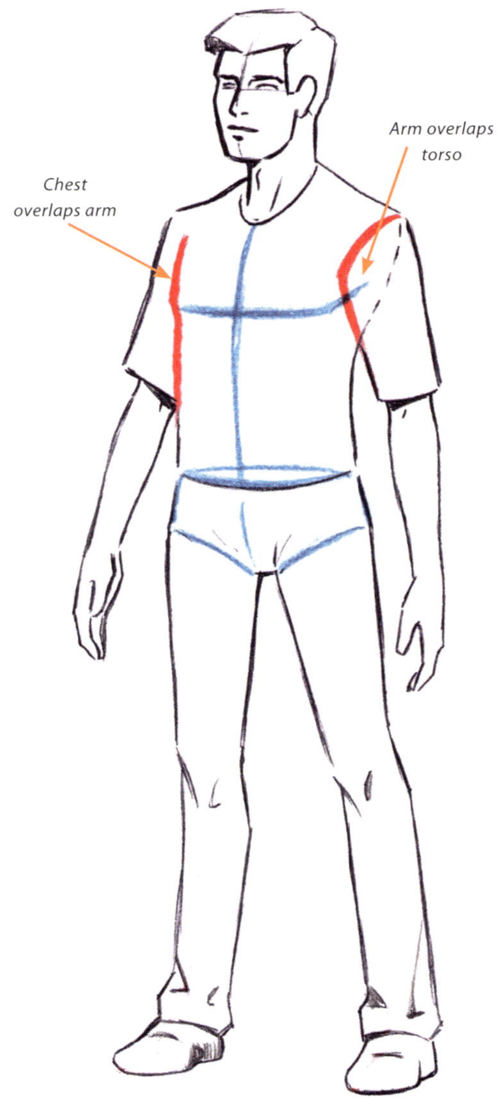

YOU TRY IT!

To create depth, practice drawing the concept of overlap in the space below.

THE BELLS AND WHISTLES

Here's another effective way to make the figure appear to have depth. We turn the back even more toward us to create what is called a three-quarter rear angle. Now we've reversed things. Instead of mostly seeing the front of the torso and a bit of the back, we are mostly seeing the back and only a bit of the torso.

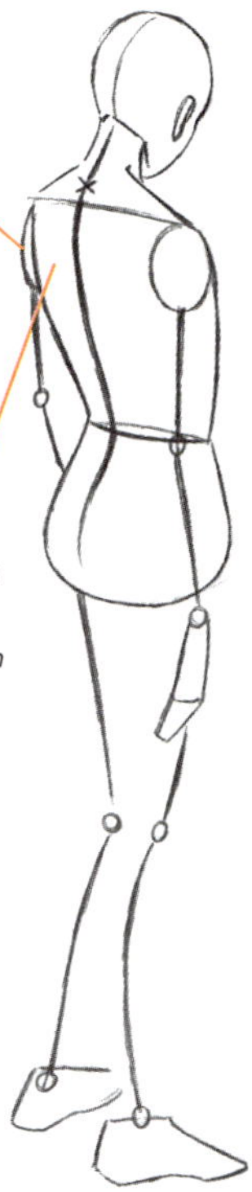

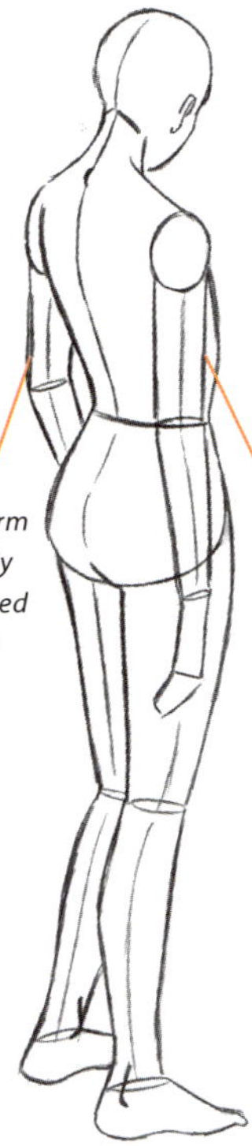

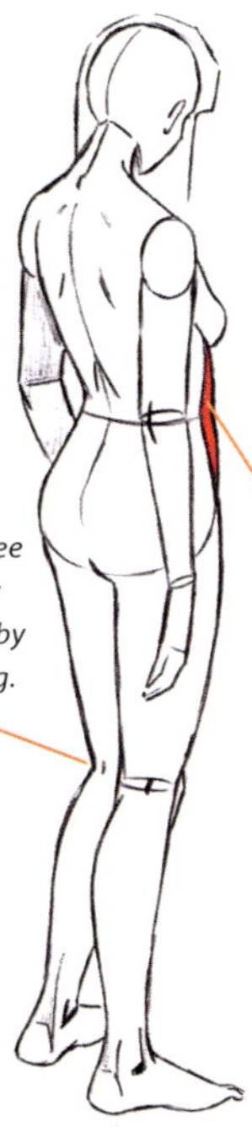

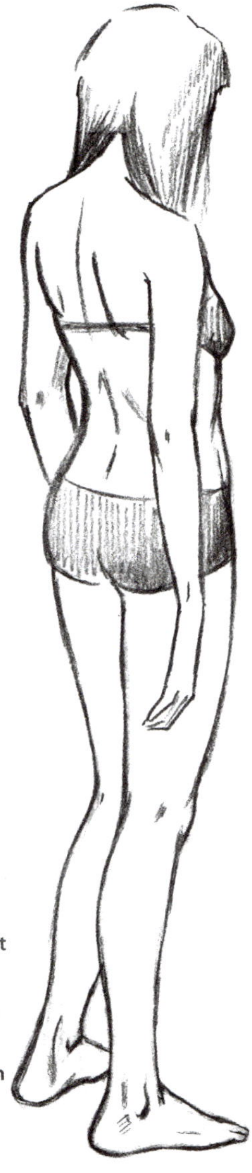

Think of the figure as having four sides: front, left side, back, right side. To show the maximum depth, show as many sides as possible to give the illusion that the viewer is seeing "around" the figure.

NOT ALL SIDES ARE OF EQUAL SIZE

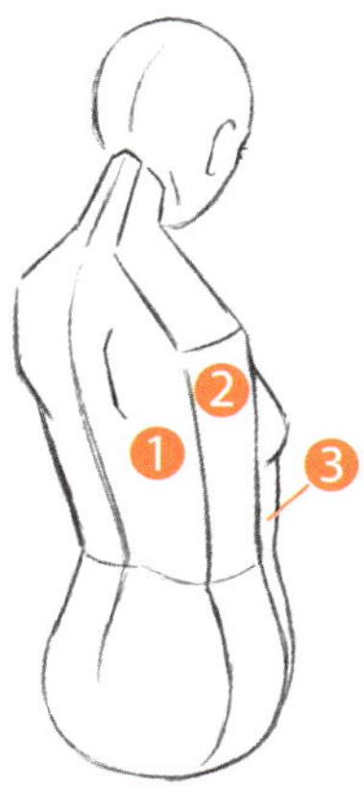

1. *In this position, the back is the primary surface.*
2. *The side of the figure is angled away from us, so it's narrower.*
3. *The front of the torso is barely visible.*

Blank pages for freehand sketching

Blank pages for freehand sketching

More Figure-Drawing Titles From

CHRISTOPHER HART

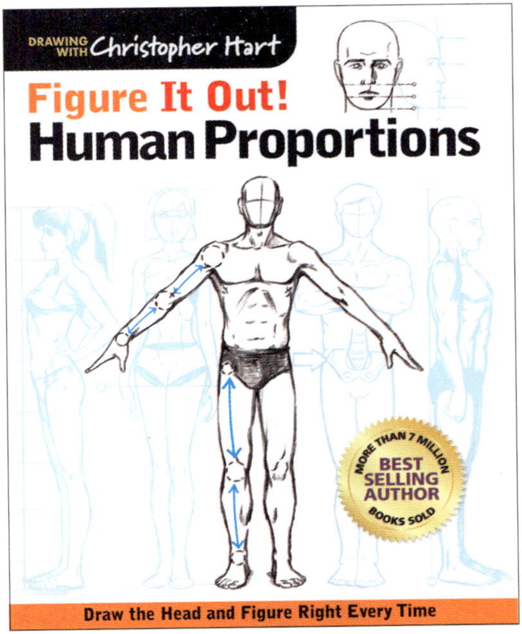

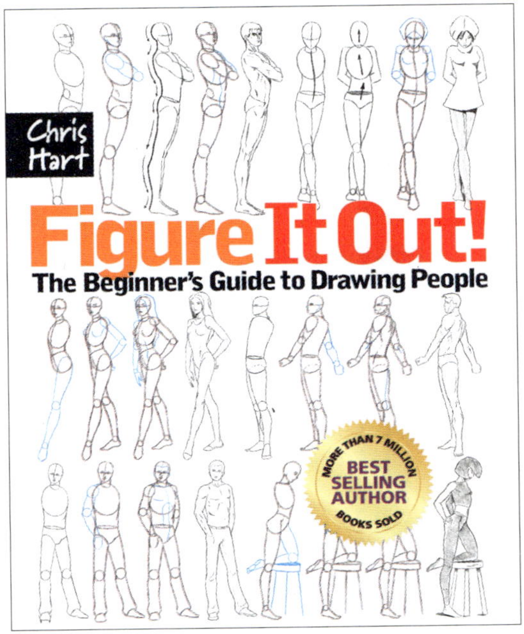

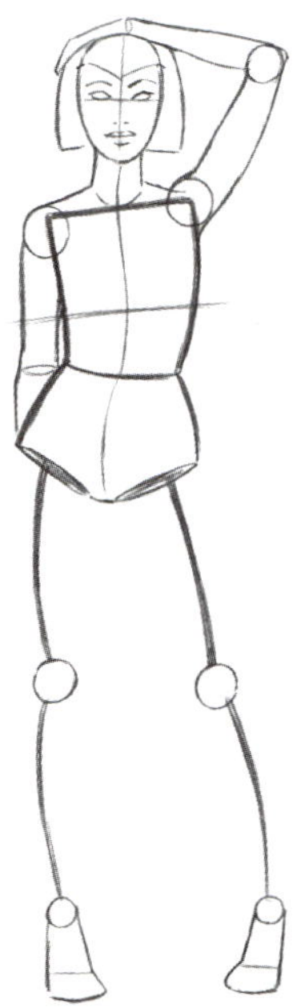

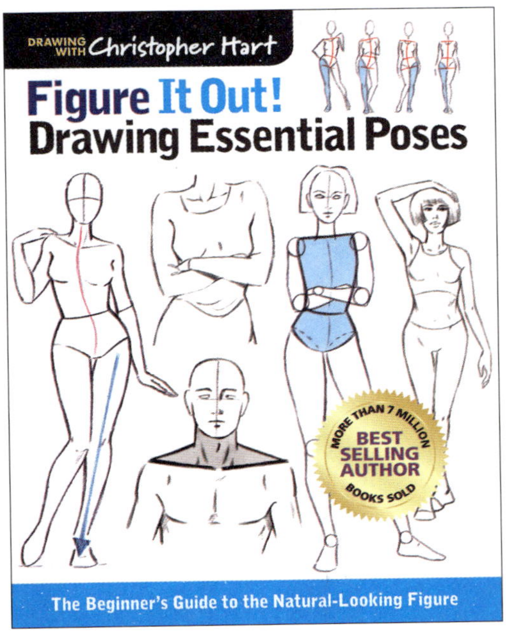

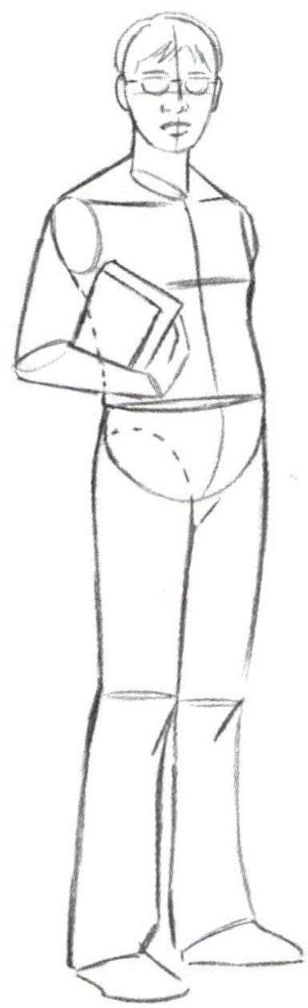